GO TO HELL

A HEATED HISTORY OF THE UNDERWORLD

By Chuck Crisafulli and Kyra Thompson

SSE

SIMON SPOTLIGHT ENTERTAINMENT

New York London Toronto Sydney

To a pair of old devils, Shine and Doc, with love

SIMON SPOTLIGHT ENTERTAINMENT
An imprint of Simon & Schuster
1230 Avenue of the Americas, New York, New York 10020
Text copyright © 2005 by Chuck Crisafulli and Kyra Thompson
All rights reserved, including the right of reproduction in whole
or in part in any form.
SIMON SPOTLIGHT ENTERTAINMENT and related logo are
trademarks of Simon & Schuster, Inc.
Designed by Yaffa Jaskoll
Manufactured in the United States of America
First Edition 10 9 8 7 6 5 4 3 2 1
Library of Congress Cataloging-in-Publication Data
Crisafulli, Chuck.
Go to hell / by Chuck Crisafulli and Kyra Thompson.— 1st ed.
p. cm.
Includes bibliographical references.

ISBN: 978-1-4767-2562-8

1. Hell. I. Thompson, Kyra. II. Title.
BL545.C75 2005
202'.3—dc22
2005010341

With grateful acknowledgment to John Rechy for granting his
permission to include his "My Hell" essay, copyright © 2005 by
John Rechy

ACKNOWLEDGMENTS

First and foremost, huge thanks to our agent, Bonnie Solow, whose unflagging dedication and enthusiasm made this trip possible. Big thanks also to Patrick Price of Simon Spotlight Entertainment for his support, understanding, and guidance. We received invaluable feedback along the way from Jacoba Atlas, Patti Crisafulli, Lex Flesher, and Nina Thompson, all of whom served as brave test readers.

We are deeply appreciative of the time, thoughts, and words we received from the special contributors to this work: Jeanine Basinger, George Dalzell, Molly Haskell, Andy Kindler, John Kricfalusi, Bob Newhart, Mark Mothersbaugh, Rosie O'Donnell, Patton Oswalt, Greg Proops, John Rechy, William Shatner, and Matt Stone.

Lastly, humble tips of the hat to Alice Turner, Elaine Pagels, and Alan Bernstein, whose works on this topic set the highest of standards for those who follow.

CONTENTS

INTRODUCTION: WHY GO TO HELL?

Abandon all hope, ye who enter here. —Dante Alighieri

Go to heaven for the climate, hell for the company. —Mark Twain

There is one immutable fact of life: It does not last forever.

And for as long as humans have been capable of pondering their own mortality, they have pondered most deeply upon one crucial question: What happens when life on earth is over?

Around the globe, throughout the centuries, across all manner of cultures and religions, the answer to this question has been twofold: We go to heaven. Or we go to hell.

The basic concept of a postearthly reward or punishment is one of the most enduring in all of human history, and it remains a bedrock tenet of faith in most modern religions. Some form of heaven is there for souls that have lived lives of essential goodness and for believers who have followed the dictates of their religion and embraced the will of their God. Hell is there to receive the darkened souls of sinners—those who have caused pain and suffering among their fellow humans and who have turned their backs on their deity.

But there is a strange corollary that accompanies this heaven/hell concept, one that has also endured through time, place, culture, and belief: Heavens have almost always been vaguely, sketchily defined as places of peace, happiness, oneness, comfort, or bliss, while hells, rife with twisted passions and bloody violence, have been meticulously mapped out almost inch by inch, with every torture and torment awaiting a condemned soul vividly imagined in excruciating detail.

Heaven has been a place where mystery is part of the appeal, a place so wonderful it is literally beyond comprehension. And perhaps humans have not wanted to jinx any chances of getting into that place by appearing to be celestial know-it-alls.

But we haven't shied away from hell. After a few thousand years of civilization, it seems fairly clear that humans have been, and remain, deeply, darkly fascinated with the place. We mortals have written about it, imagined it, painted it, filmed it, dreamt it, and debated its very existence with a level of specificity and a degree of passion rarely mustered in considering "the better place."

It would seem that we humans want desperately to end up in heaven. But in the meantime, we can't get enough of hell.

Maybe that's because, by nature, we feel a little closer to hell. Heaven is a place of perfected spirit. Hell is the final destination for corrupted flesh. There aren't too many of us who walk around feeling perfect, but just about everybody can think of a fleshly stumble or two to call their own. We may not be certain who the angels among us are, but we sure as hell can spot the wicked. And so hell—from religion to religion and century to century—has become a landscape where all our darkest, basest, most corrupted impulses run rampant. In Hollywood-speak, hell has proven to have some legs: it's got conflict, drama, villains, sex, violence, fire, darkness, torment, and ultimate justice—everything we might demand and expect of our late-night entertainment.

Which raises another interesting twist in hell's history. For as long as the place has been a focus of fear, it's also been a setting for wicked fun. Homer's descriptions of Hades in the *Odyssey* weren't intended as religious instruction; they were rip-roaring adventure tales.

The mystery plays of the Middle Ages often made hell a crowd-pleasing showcase of vulgar slapstick. And today, when many of us still believe in hell as a very real place of final, eternal punishment, we can still root for a "Demons" sports team or watch an actor dressed as the devil hawk a brand of spicy salsa without feeling our souls are in particular peril. The proverbial Martian glancing upon our culture-in-general would observe that the hell we might hear about in churches coexists in an oddly symbiotic fashion with the hell of horror movies, heavy metal bands, video games, *New Yorker* cartoons, *South Park*, and pizzerias with "Inferno" in their names.

It is in that mixed spirit of fear and fascination that we have assembled our chapter-by-chapter tour of hell. This work isn't intended as a soberly academic one. And it's not a heavy-duty study of comparative religion. Our goal has been to offer up a layperson's look at the way hell has been imagined and reimagined over time, and across cultures and religions. The work also takes a look at the way hell has been able to serve seemingly contradictory roles, as both the scariest after-earth destination imaginable for human souls, and as one of the deepest and richest sources of art and entertainment for those very same souls while they're still earthbound. We've tried to balance a fairly thorough examination of hell's religious history with a more playful look at its shifting significance as a fixture of pop culture around the globe and through the centuries.

As a part of our look at hell's heated presence in pop culture, we've included throughout the book some segments titled "My Hell." These are varied, brief, personal thoughts on hell's makeup, drawn from our interviews with a mix of creative folks from the worlds of film, television, books, music, and academia (and ranging from the generally beloved to the decidedly controversial). Their responses are meant to play off a larger point: Our world's ongoing, unsettled religious and philosophical debates on the nature of hell indicate that the place below might still be considered a work in progress, continually reshaped, restoked, and reconsidered by all humans still interested in pondering life's imponderables.

To be honest, for those with a devout sense of faith, this book may be entirely beside the point. If a believer already has a strong sense of the singular truth, the last thing he or she needs is a postmodern, pan-religious, omnicultural history of hell to muck things up. And yet that history is out there, dynamic and undeniable, and we feel it is a history worthy of at least some investigation. It is a strange, eventful history that is by turns grand, fearsome, comic, mortifying, and always wickedly compelling. In laying out our look at hell, we've attempted to stay true to the blend of tragedy and comedy that has marked discussions of the place since such discussions began millennia ago. It has been our sincere desire to do justice to the seriousness of the subject, while acknowledging that hell is a subject that mortals have not always taken so seriously.

With the understanding of just how remarkable, significant, and influential a place hell is, the intention of *Go to Hell* is not to dismiss the netherworld, but to illuminate it just a bit. The hope has been to create a book that's engagingly readable, rather than one that's simply damnable.

WHAT THE HELL IS HELL?

Hell is murky! —Shakespeare, *Macbeth*
If you're going through hell, keep going. —Winston Churchill

Hot and horrible. But not always.

A place below us. But is it a real place?

A mythological construct. But for souls suffering eternal damnation, it may not feel so "mythological."

Perhaps it can be assumed that we'll know it when we see it, but in the meantime, what the hell, precisely, is hell?

A clear, basic definition, which has held up from era to era and religion to religion, is this: Hell is a separation from God. If a religion's God represents all that is good and right in the cosmos, then hell is the state of being in which a soul is completely and utterly shunned from the presence of God.

There is certainly something elegant about defining hell as an absence, in considering it to be a realm defined by the impossibility of joy and fulfillment, rather than as a realm defined by damnation and shriek-making torment. But it's a definition that also feels incomplete. To be sure, "separation from God" sounds terrible and terrifying—the ultimate, shameful punishment for the God-defying mortal. But we mortals have spent a few millennia energetically believing in much more detailed visions of what hell might be.

Fire. Brimstone. Gleefully malicious demons. Rending of flesh. Circles of escalating agonies.

These sorts of hellish images spring just as readily to mind when we think of the place, upping our fears with a sharp prod to the viscera.

Then again, even as we've worriedly hungered for details on the nature of hell, there's been an odd tension in the way we consider and speak of the netherworld. Hell has to be considered the most frightening place we could find ourselves in—a terrible, inescapable punishment for a badly lived life. If we take its existence seriously, there's not much to do but shudder in fear and pray to our God that we are living a life that qualifies us for a better place. But, even as centuries' worth of such prayers have been offered up, hell has a concurrent history in which it has been a realm of imagination. It's been a setting for story-telling that allows indulgence of all our unspeakable thoughts and passions. It's been the dramatic backdrop for darkest satire, grand comeuppances, grisly narratives, and cautionary tales.

Certainly it's a nasty place that no one wants to call home, but that hasn't stopped centuries of humans from wanting to take a peek through some nether windows to see just how wicked the wicked are, and to perhaps experience the satisfaction of cosmic schadenfreude when we discover how exactly the wicked among us are dealt with ("Ah, yes—just what they deserved").

For many, hell is an unquestionably real place in which human sins will be judged and punished with severe finality. For others, it's a not-so-real place in which all of our human foibles and frailties are resignedly recognized, and even perversely celebrated.

So then, how did such a place come to be?

What the hell is hell?

Well, it's important to note that at the beginning of hell's history the place wasn't always so hot, it wasn't always so bad, and it didn't always last forever. Before the hell of eternal damnation was established, there was simply the "underworld," a place where dead souls wandered. Belief in this kind of neutral underworld spanned cultures and centuries, from the Mesopotamians to the ancient Chinese to the Aztecs. Early Israelites believed in Sheol, a version of the afterlife described as a shadowy underground in which all souls, regardless of their inherent good or evil, lived on in dusty, perpetual thirst. In Eastern religions, belief in reincarnation meant that hell, rather than being a place of eternal torment, was more akin to a horrible temp job: You put in your time burning off the ugly sins of one life and get ready for another go at living a good life.

The idea that hell could serve a double purpose as religious reality and an entertainment vehicle was right there from the start too, as evidenced by the prototypical underworld narrative found in the epic tale of Gilgamesh, which chronicles a death-fearing king's search for immortality. From a modern perspective, it's admittedly hard to get a clear idea of the audience expectations and collective, common-denominator sense of humor of ancient Mesopotamia ("Three Sumerians walk into a Phoenician beer parlor . . ."), but the wild exploits of Gilgamesh seem to unfold as a crowd-pleasing summer blockbuster of its time.

Nonpunitive underworlds gradually turned darker and nastier, and judgment became a more prominent part of Land of the Dead proceedings. Early Judaic beliefs were influential in the initial conception of hell as a place of banishment and fiery torment, though since the eighteenth century Judaism has rejected the idea of hell and damnation as concepts that are contrary to the nature of God. It was a sixth-century B.C. Persian prophet, Zoroaster, who first began to articulate a notion of a monotheistic, good-versus-evil duality that would be reflected in the afterlife. His writing greatly informed the Christian and Muslim beliefs that followed, and many modern images of hell trace directly back to the vision of a netherworld first propounded in Zoroastrian teachings.

When did the fire start? Where did the demons come from? What the heck is brimstone?

For some answers, let's begin by slipping into some underworlds.

DOWN, BUT NOT DAMNED

It actually took quite a while for hell to become fully hellish. As humans began to puzzle out the intriguing concept of a human soul that lived on after the flesh, so too did they develop the idea of a nonjudgmental netherworld in which these souls were collected. Consequently, almost all ancient cultures had some belief in an underworld that served not as a place of eternal damnation or final punishment but simply as a Land of the Dead or Great Below—the place a soul descended to when the flesh gave up its last breath and became an ungainly source of fertilizer.

Between four and five thousand years ago, the ancient cultures of Mesopotamia—Sumerians, Phoenicians, Assyrians, Babylonians—all developed the belief that the Land of the Dead was a subterranean world where all mortal souls eventually resided regardless of lifetimes of good or bad behavior; while the heavens above the earthly world were considered to be the exclusive realm of those cultures' rosters of gods.

There seems to have been a good deal of mixing and matching of gods and legends as these civilizations constructed their respective underworld mythos. Many precise details of belief have been lost over the millennia, but in the numerous surviving cuneiform tablets of the Babylonians, a vivid picture of hell as a real place emerges.

The Babylonian hell of Kurnugia was far beneath the ground, but not so far that both gods and mortals couldn't travel back and forth between earth and the underworld (thus beginning the tradition of "visits to hell" storytelling that carries right through from the

Harrowing of Hell narratives of the Middle Ages to the near-death-experience hell visions of contemporary times). But rather than serving as a setting for the perils of damnation, Kurnugia was envisioned primarily as a setting for the wild exploits and unpredictable behavior of visiting gods—a kind of netherworldly VIP lounge.

MAP CHECK

For the record, Mesopotamia covered what we now know as Iraq. Mesopotamia is a Greek word for "between rivers," the rivers in this case being the Tigris and Euphrates.

Overseeing the comings and goings at Kurnugia was a very powerful female. In an early though short-lived demonstration of underworldly gender equality, the tempestuous proto-hell was ruled by Ereshkigal, the Babylonian princess of the kingdom of shadows. She was a creature of great power, though not exactly a shining role model for Babylonian girls—she's moody, violent, jealous, and not above using some energetic underworld sex to get what she's after (namely, some decent underworld companionship).

Life in this underworld wasn't all that different from life in the real world. The inhabitants—including gods, demigods, and mortals—all had to worry about securing food, water, clothing, and material goods, and were all subject to shifting positions of status. There was a fair amount of dreariness in Kurnugia, and many of the consigned dead souls had nothing to do but sit in dust and darkness wearing bird costumes, no doubt feeling like attendees at the worst stadium mascots' convention ever. (Why birds? The legends don't make that clear, but it is a feathery image that will be echoed by Lucifer's fallen angels.)

But Kurnugia isn't truly a place of final judgment or punishment; as a Land of the Dead, it's more often a generator of excitingly lurid stories, a melodramatic hotbed of jealousy and ambition, lust and violence. The setting for a soap opera of the gods.

The damnation's not there yet, but the titillation is, and that helps heat things up for hells to come.

A FINE GILGAMESH

One of the oldest recorded stories in the world comes from some nearly four-thousand-year-old clay tablets of

Mesopotamian origin. That story is the epic tale of Gilgamesh, a Sumerian hero-king who may or may not have actually existed. The story of Gilgamesh is important hellwise for a couple of reasons. First, his tale lays out some of the basic and enduring elements of underworlds and hells that followed. Second, the driving motivation behind the Gilgamesh narrative would become a guiding force for many visions of hell to come: the fear of death.

In short, King Gilgamesh is freaked out by the thought of his own mortality, and heads off through twelve tablets' worth of strange adventures in order to come to terms with his eventual demise.

Gilgamesh's problems stem chiefly from the fact that he is not a very well-liked ruler of the kingdom of Uruk. Yes, he's strong and good-looking, but among his kingly duties he has claimed the right to celebrate every bride's wedding night by having sex with her before the groom does. Sure, it's more personal than a toast, but the practice understandably begins to grate on the nerves of Uruk's husbands and husbands-to-be. Gilgamesh's subjects appeal to the gods for some justice, and the gods respond by creating an equally powerful adversary for the king: a wild, animal-loving mountain man named Enkidu. At first, Enkidu is content to live the simple wild life among his animal friends, but the gods send a tainted harlot his way to seduce him and tell him about Gilgamesh. ("Tainted" isn't simply a moral judgment here. After the harlot and Enkidu hook up for a week of lovemaking, Enkidu's wild animal friends can sniff the difference in their buddy and won't associate with him any longer.)

With the encouragements of the harlot, Enkidu decides to head to Uruk to face off with Gilgamesh. And Enkidu knows just how to get the king's attention, blocking Gilgamesh from entering the boudoir of another new bride. Enkidu and Gilgamesh go through some fierce male bonding—they beat the crap out of each other—and then, with the logic of so many future buddy movies, they quickly become best friends. They decide to make a name for themselves by doing a bit of rambling together, and for kicks, they set off to slaughter the guardian monster of a cedar forest.

The successful slaughtering captures the attention of the ever-comely and ever-game Inanna, goddess of love. She attempts to seduce Gilgamesh, but he declines her offer of casual sex, unwisely reminding her of all the ex-lovers she has left dead, destroyed, or otherwise full of heartache (one ex-bedmate was turned into a frog, for instance). The goddess complains to her dad, the extremely powerful god Anu, and pretty soon the full pantheon of gods is demanding that either Gilgamesh or Enkidu has to die for the double crime of not properly servicing Inanna and being an arrogant jerk.

Gilgamesh has been under the impression that since his own mom was a goddess, he is immortal. But it turns out that he inherited his life force from his human father's side of the family: He is quite mortal and can indeed be killed. This is not news he accepts gracefully, and his consternation isn't much dimmed when the gods pick Enkidu as the one to be snuffed. Gilgamesh reaches a state of high anxiety as he watches his friend die and decompose; then he sets out to find the one guy he thinks can help him— a fellow with the not exactly melodious name of Utnapishtim, the only mortal ever granted eternal life by the gods. Gilgamesh believes that this is the guy who can tell him the secrets of death, particularly how to avoid it.

DOWN UNDER

Gilgamesh then begins a journey through an underworld that includes many signature features of later hells. There's darkness. There are caverns. There is a gateway guarded by a strange creature (in this case, a half man/half scorpion). There's a body of water that must be crossed. And there's a mysterious boatman who offers the only way to get across it.

Not everything is recognizably hellish. Gilgamesh also encounters a friendly female underworld winemaker, who offers up a bit of exuberant life-coaching ("Let your clothes be fresh, bathe yourself in water, cherish the little child that holds your hand, and make your wife happy in your embrace . . .").

Gilgamesh finally meets up with Utnapishtim, whose very detailed, tablets' worth of backstory is strikingly similar to that of Noah and the Flood in the book of Genesis. The immortal mortal and his wife end up pitying the death-obsessed traveler-king, and generously share with him a plant that will keep him young. Then in what seems a bit of a forced plot twist, Gilgamesh promptly loses the plant to a hungry snake that slithers by in the water just when he is taking up that friendly winemaker's advice about bathing.

But upon returning to Uruk, Gilgamesh ultimately calms the hell down and achieves a measure of death acceptance. Looking at the greatness of his castle and the small pleasures of everyday life all around him, he decides he'll try to live a good life rather than an unending one.

A BRIEF GLOSSARY OF HELL-SPEAK

Hellacious: disgusting, extraordinary, or both.

Hellion: a troublemaker.

Hell-raiser: one given to boisterous, extreme behavior.

Hell to pay: a bad result. From the nautical usage of "to pay," meaning "to waterproof by covering with pitch or tar." Obviously, waterproofing hell is not a job one wants to find oneself stuck with.

Snowball's chance in hell: no chance at all.

When hell freezes over: never.

Going to hell in a handbasket: seems to be an alteration of "to heaven in a handbasket," the idea being that, in either direction, the task is accomplished very easily.

BOOK-OF-THE-DEAD CLUB

The basic dynamic of the Mesopotamian prehell under-world was echoed in the underworld of another ascendant power of the day, Egypt. For the ancient Egyptians, the underworld was located far beneath the earthly realm and was also a neutral place of wandering dead souls and godly melodrama. Egyptian scholars and clerics circa 2000 B.C. recorded much of their thinking on death and the afterlife in the Egyptian Book of the Dead.

The book consists of chapters pulled from Pyramid Texts—the hieroglyphics carved inside Pyramid walls— as well as later writings that were carved directly into the deceased's wooden coffin, the appropriately named Coffin Texts. The book evolved over fifteen centuries and grew to include a number of otherworldly spells and incantations that were written down on sheets of papyrus. Along the way, Egyptian beliefs morphed from a kind of active day-to-day religion, in which a variety of gods were intimately involved in everyday life, to a general, large-scale undergirding for a theocratic state. (There was no Egyptian equivalent of the Bible or the Koran, and eventually the will of the gods could only be made clear through the pronouncements of the pharaoh and his ruling-class priests.)

But some of the basic beliefs held fairly steady across those centuries, including the vision of an underworld. As the Book of the Dead made clear, the knowable universe was divided into the three realms of heaven, earth, and an expansive underworld called Duat. Duat, very much like Kurnugia, was not conceived as a place of punishment, but it was not pleasant, often described by turns as numbingly gloomy and terrifyingly perilous. The dead would hope to get through the difficulties of Duat to reach a smaller, happier terrain within: the blissful, heavenly Field of Rushes (sometimes translated as the Field of Reeds).

The Egyptians were obsessed with the idea of immortality, and when they put together the Book of the Dead, what they were actually writing was a book *for* the dead. The spells, prayers, secret passwords, directions, warnings, and advice carved into those Pyramids and coffins were for the benefit of the dead soul—that is, a soul wealthy or respected enough to have justified the expense of a Pyramid or coffin. The writings provided the newly dead with both a road map and a pep talk on its dangerous journey through the underworld.

RA-RA-RA

One of the most powerful Egyptian underworld heavyweights was the sun god Ra. Heavyweight enough to be worshipped by his own cult and to have Pyramids and special solar temples constructed in his honor, Ra is a pivotal figure in many Egyptian creation myths, but, as active sun god, he spends just about half his time in the underworld—from sunset until the next day's sunrise. Duat was the place Ra repaired to each evening when he departed the sky after a hard day's sun-toting and soul-hauling (part of his job was to bring the freshly dead to the underworld). But post-tote rest and relaxation did not come easy down below.

Despite being a powerful god, Ra found himself besieged and assaulted by a variety of enemies and mal-contents each time he descended to the underworld. Perhaps his most formidable adversary was Apep, a grotesque, oversized serpent who desired nothing more than to swallow up Ra and the sun-ship the god sailed on (Apep's also sometimes referred to as a dragon). Ra had to do fierce battle with the creature each night as he journeyed through Duat, but as each day's rising sun would attest, the god usually won out (a stormy, overcast day might mean that Apep was putting up a fiercer fight than usual). In some Ra tales, the god actually goes through a cycle of creation each day, dying in the underworld and then being reborn in time to start a new day. Another interesting detail that emerges in some Pyramid hieroglyphics is that the souls lurking about in Duat are always happy to have Ra sail through the underworld, because as sun god he lightens things up a bit. When he leaves each morning to light the earthly sky, the place plunges back into gloominess.

LET'S DUAT AGAIN

The Egyptians developed the idea that the soul was split into two significant, interdependent components. There was the "Ba," the physical shell of the body that had to remain pure and intact after death. This was accomplished through the rituals of mummification the ancients are famous for—effective, reverential treatment of the Ba is what has allowed King Tutankhamen a career of sellout appearances thirty-three centuries after his untimely demise. The Ba also had to be supplied with all the material goods necessary for a comfortable afterlife: food, drink, weapons, toiletries, and plenty of luxury items (thus the trove of treasures often found in a mummy's tomb).

There was also the "Ka," a kind of spirit doppelgänger that did the actual voyaging into the underworld. The Ka's journey began with a boat ride courtesy of sun god Ra, who dutifully carted his daily cargo of the freshly dead across the river of the sky to the final point of disembarkation: Duat. The Duat was described as a dark, forbidding landscape of desert and scrubland, with a few even darker forests here and there. One of the first things a nervous Ka might've noticed was that there were no clear roads leading anywhere. It was impossible for the disembodied soul to find its way through the bleak wilderness without the guidance of the Book of the Dead or some advice from friendly inhabitants. Friendly inhabitants weren't so easy to come by, however—most locals tended to be more along the lines of giant, ravenous crocodiles, flesh-eating scarab beetles, unsympathetic water snakes, or malevolent spirit creatures who had to be bribed for directions. In addition to these perils, the Ka might find itself suddenly cursed into a state of being able to walk only upside down, or cursed further into a state of relying on its own excrement as its only supply of trail mix.

Assuming that the Ka was smart and worthy enough to avoid the monsters of Duat and figure out where it was going, it would make its way through a series of seven gates, each manned by a crew of surly, powerful gatekeepers. Like some intrepid nightclubber trying to make his way past increasingly daunting velvet ropes and increasingly monstrous bouncers, the Ka had to properly acknowledge each gate's crew with special chants and passwords from the Book of the Dead and hope they were enough to get it through ("Hey, I'm a close friend of Ra's! He said it'd be cool . . .").

MY HELL

WILLIAM SHATNER
Actor, author, Starfleet captain

Hell, for me, would be to leave here today.
  Right now.
  Maybe tomorrow—that would be all right.
  But not today.
  I'm having too much fun.
  And to leave right now . . . ?
  That would be hell.

HERE COMES THE JUDGMENT

It is in the Egyptian underworld that we first see the idea of the judgment of a soul. While everyone heads off to the same underworld in the same fashion, Osiris, god of the dead, makes a judgment regarding where that soul will ultimately end up. (Souls that didn't make it to Osiris—by way of an improperly maintained Ba or a crocodile-consumed Ka—were reincarnated back to a life on earth.)

The Ka that made it to Osiris's realm, Sekhet-Hetepet, would be accosted by Anubis, Osiris's jackal-headed son, whose official underworld role was that of "psychopomp," or conductor of the souls. Anubis would lead the way to a Hall of Justice, where without much prep time, the Ka would find itself summarily put on trial before Osiris. The Ka was in the position of defending the life of the mortal from which it had departed, and pleading for a happy spot in the heavenly Field of Rushes.

Courtroom skills mattered less than simple cardio weight, however: Anubis placed a soul's heart on the Scales of Judgment and weighed it against a Feather of Truth. If the organ meat and the feather balanced out: Hello, Rushes. But if the heart outweighed the feather, it was clearly chubbied up with wickedness and sin, and the despondent, fat-hearted sinner was immediately pounced upon by the grotesque and voracious monster Ammut, eater of the dead.

SHUT YER HELLMOUTH

It's worth spending an extra moment with the insatiably hungry, unspeakably ugly Ammut because he represents an image that goes on to become an awfully powerful one in hell's history—that of the hellmouth. Ammut was a portly, unsightly mix of lion, crocodile, and hippo parts, and the worst thing that could happen to a soul was that it would be gulped up by this beast to spend eternity in its innards. Hell is most often conceived of as a place that one descends to, but here's a more frightening twist: hell as a snack-loving monster that can pursue you and devour you in a single slurp. The notion of hell as a hungry beast waiting—Great White–like—to chomp you into eternal damnation is not one that carried through explicitly in religious beliefs, but it became a significant bit of hell imagery. In medieval artwork, the devil's throne often had gnashing, soul-hungry jaws with which to consume the damned. In the mystery and miracle plays of the Middle Ages, the hellmouth was a particularly crucial bit of scenery, often taking the form of a huge, open-jawed demon head placed over a trapdoor. Renaissance puppet-theater productions weren't complete without a hellmouth to swallow up the vilest papier-mâché souls. And, of course, a variation of hellmouth survived powerfully into modern times beneath the otherwise pleasant burg of Sunnydale, home of hardworking Buffy the Vampire Slayer.

BUFFED OUT

One particular hellmouth enjoyed seven seasons' worth of prime-time, high-profile exposure as a plot-generating, malevolent point of interest beneath the otherwise bland, generically Southern Californian town of Sunnydale, the setting of *Buffy the Vampire Slayer*. For those unfamiliar with the work of the intrepid young Buffy, the general mythology behind her show went something like this:

In the early 1900s, a centuries-old, extremely powerful vampire called "the Master" attempted to open up Hellmouth, the better to unleash untold forces of evil. But in the process of his Grand Opening ritual in an abandoned church, a pesky Southern Californian earthquake struck, leaving the vampire in the embarrassing position of being trapped for decades in a collapsed holy place. The Master finds himself up against an ultimate adversary when Sunnydale also becomes the adopted home of LA native Buffy Anne Summers, who, as a high school freshman, has learned that she is a Chosen One, a slayer of extraordinary powers who is destined to battle the scourge of demons and vampires attempting to wreak havoc with humanity.

After years of fighting off such nemeses as snake monsters, sewer monsters, undead art dealers, blood-thirsty cheerleaders, skin-eating demons, a student-eating mayor, and increasingly crafty vampires—not to mention dealing with her own death and resurrection—Buffy and her allies overpower the forces of evil and, in an Emmy-nominated display of special effects, watch in awe as the hellmouth collapses in on itself, devouring Sunnydale in the process.

Buffy ends there, but the slayer's work may not be done—a couple of episodes of the series contain references to a hellmouth sitting under Cleveland.

BIGMOUTH ON PARADE

The city of Chester in northwest England was famous throughout medieval and Tudor times for its Midsummer Watch Parade, a massive spectacle put on in the June of years when the city's mystery play was not being staged. The parade, a form of puppet theater on a grand scale, featured appropriately gigantic puppets of a family of Giants, as well as supersized Giant Beasts (unicorn, camel, elephant, and dragon) and an assortment of angels, devils, and fiery goblins. In 1995, after a three-hundred-plus-year hiatus, Chester revived its parade tradition, and the whole community proudly pitched in to reconstruct a Giant family, new beasts, and one other crucial element of the parade: a huge, mobile hellmouth.

BACK EAST

The major Eastern religions never focused sharply on the concept of reward or punishment in an eternal afterlife, and so did not place as great an emphasis on the idea of a singular hell to be feared. In both Buddhism and Hinduism, the soul goes through many cycles of reincarnation, so hells are places of penitence, even torment, but they are blessedly temporary. A soul passes through hell to work off the sins of one life before beginning the next. While the manner in which a soul is processed through these hells is sometimes rendered in excruciating detail,

the places themselves are not given much substance—
these hells tend to exist in a spirit dimension quite apart
from our world.

BAD DOWN BELOW (BUT YOU DON'T HAVE TO GO)

In ancient Japan, the religion of Shintoism developed as
a system of folk beliefs and traditions; it wasn't based
upon any sacred texts or holy scriptures. The underly-
ing principle in Shinto beliefs was that the natural
world was made up of a variety of spirits called "kami."
Kami were behind all the natural processes of the world:
They made the wind blow, the sun shine, and the plants
bloom, and they oversaw almost every element of life
and death. The pleasant news in Shintoism was that
there was no hell, and that everyone would eventually
upon death become a kami. But Shintoists were not
blind to the fact that bad things happened on earth, and
so they came to believe that in addition to the kami,
there were evil spirits at work that brought disease,
pestilence, and misfortune to humans. These spirits
dwelled underground in a place called Yomi-tsu-kuni,

the land of darkness. Drought, flood, fire, accidents—
these were all the works of the spiteful spirits of Yomi-
tsu-kuni, and they were taken as proof that this shadowy netherworld was a very real place. Yomi-tsu-kuni
could be accessed by a long, twisting, difficult road, but
there wasn't much reason to make that trip—the place
was believed to be as unpleasant and forbidding as the
spirits that inhabited it.

BOOK-OF-THE-DEAD CLUB II

Like the ancient Egyptians, Tibetan Buddhists also developed a body of advice and guidance to be passed along
to departing spirits, the Bardo Thodol, or *The Tibetan Book
of the Dead*. The knowledge eventually contained within
the book was passed along orally for many centuries
before actually taking book form in the eighth century
A.D. through the writings of Padmasambhava, aka Guru
Rinpoche, the founder of the tantric school of Buddhism.

The Tibetan book differed in some significant
ways from the Egyptian equivalent. While the Egyptian
book was meant to be used as a reference work by a
spirit that had left its body, the Bardo Thodol was

meant to be read by the living to a person in the process of dying. A great deal of importance was placed on the precise moment of death, when a properly coached spirit could find its way to liberation and reincarnation. An uncoached spirit might knock about in a state of utter afterlife confusion.

In the Tibetan Book of the Dead, hell is a period of time after death that lasts forty-nine days, the length of time it takes for a soul to leave the dying person and become incarnated in a womb for its next life. Even with such a finite end in sight, hell time isn't a walk in the afterworld park. Within those forty-nine days, a soul may encounter impenetrable darkness, wild animals, avalanches, hurricanes, bottomless pits, and heavily armed, flesh-eating demons. The soul may also suffer vicious dismemberment at the hands of Yama, lord of death (though the soul is advised not to panic as it is carved up, as its body doesn't actually exist anymore). Recognizing that some souls may need a little moral support in making it through the full forty-nine days, the Tibetan Book of the Dead helpfully provides prayers for the living to continue reading for a departed soul, so that they may act as a kind of home-team cheering section to help guide the confused soul through its perplexing torments.

FLIPPING THE BIRD

Some Indian branches of Buddhism developed longer periods of penitence and punishment. There might be a variety of hells that a soul could be assigned to, and in each case that hell is to be endured in the space between death and rebirth. The period of time served is measured in fragments of "kalpas," and while a kalpa might not sound like much and a fragment might sound even more encouraging, this hell time does not pass quickly. In Buddhist texts, kalpas are cycles of creation, and they are varyingly described as totaling up to anywhere from tens of millions to hundreds of millions to billions of years. Some early Buddhist teachers used an analogy to get the point across: Imagine a mountain of rock a mile high, a mile wide, and a mile long. Once a day, a rather complacent bird flies by and gives that mountain a peck with its beak. Think of how long it would take for that bird to turn that mountain into nothing more than a stretch of fine sand. That's a kalpa. (An alternate analogy has the mountain being rubbed once a day with a piece of silk—when the mountain's rubbed away, you've got a kalpa).

MIRROR, MIRROR

By the sixth century A.D., Buddhism had become a potent force in Japan, and with it came a forbidding vision of the netherworld. Japanese Buddhists believed in the existence of a dark realm called Jigoku, which consisted of a series of sixteen separate hells far beneath the earth, each tailored to properly punish a sinner before the soul advances to a heavenly plane. Like an all-you-can-suffer hot-and-cold buffet, Jigoku contained eight fiery hells and eight icy hells. All were ruled over by a single Great Judge of Hell, the berobed Emma-O, who, in the event of any postmortal misbehavior, had the Oni—an army of miscreant demons—to back him up.

Jigoku had a couple of darkly ingenious features. First, Emma-O, like the Egyptians' Osiris, had the ability to weigh a soul to find out just how much wickedness it had accumulated. Second, arguing with that scale was always going to be a losing battle, because the Judge also possessed a fantastic mirror that did not reflect a soul's physical appearance, but instead reflected all the thoughts, words, actions (and, obviously, sins) that had made up the soul's existence. ("I never stole a thing in my life," cries the soul. "Take a look into this mirror, and please explain to us precisely what your neighbor's ivory snuffbox is doing in your pocket," says Emma-O. "Oh, that. Heh-heh . . ." Nailed!)

THE SPINS

The Buddhist beliefs of ancient China also sent a soul through a fairly complex, nether-judicial system of Courts of Hell. The soul descended through a complicated network of caverns to arrive at the coldly officious reception area, where a reckoning commenced. A soul judged to be of unimpeachable virtue would sidestep the rest of the underworld judicial process and ascend to the reward of a place in paradise. A few lucky souls wandering through the caverns of hell might encounter Ti-Tsang Wang, a smiling god of mercy who gave up his own position in paradise in order to liberate souls from hell. But most souls with a heavy burden of sins to work off had to pass through the remaining, and extremely punishing, Courts of Hell, spending enough time in each to be cleansed of whatever particular bad behaviors they had been judged guilty of (everything from dishonesty to murder was covered).

The soul proceeded until it reached the final court, where it was mounted on a wheel of transmigration and spun back into a new life of physical existence and another shot at living a good life. As trips through hell were part of the eternal cycle of life and death, birth and rebirth, Vegas house rules did not apply: A single soul got as many earth lives and wheel spins as it took to live a life pure enough to win entrance to paradise.

HOWDY DUALITY

Not much is known about the life of sixth-century B.C. Persian prophet Zoroaster. Even calling him a sixth-century B.C. prophet named named Zoroaster may be a little off because guesstimates of his actual birth date range over the course of a thousand years, and *Zoroaster* is a Greek translation of the prophet's actual name, Zarathustra (which translates into English as "golden camel," "golden light," or "golden star," depending on who's doing the translating). But even while biographical data remain sketchy, it's clear that this poet and religious thinker had a tremendous influence, not only as the founder of a powerfully unifying, monotheistic

Middle Eastern religion, but also as a shaper of the religions (and by extension, the hells) that developed after his time.

Zoroaster laid out his religious vision in a series of hymns and teachings called the Gathas, which were eventually collected into the holy book of Zoroastrianism, the Avesta. The Big Idea of Zoroastrianism was this: enough already with all the different gods of this and that, some good, some bad, some good or bad depending on mood. And forget about everybody heading for the same underworld. There's a force of light and there's a force of darkness, and every soul will be irrevocably judged to fit with one side or the other.

The appeal of Zoroaster's vision was that it streamlined traditional beliefs and created an easily graspable, easily teachable, ultimate duel of duality: good versus evil.

Zoroaster's singular god was Ahura Mazda, the wise creator of heaven and earth. The evil opposition party was led by Ahriman, a powerful spirit of lies, pride, and bad thoughts. Mortals live out their lives in a constant struggle to choose which of the two examples to follow. The common underworld of previous religions is reduced to a single bridge, the Chinvato Peretu, and as a newly dead soul begins to cross the bridge, its entire life's worth of thoughts and actions are tallied up. If the math works out so that the good of a soul outweighs the evil, the soul earns a ticket across the bridge to heaven. But if the evil outweighs the good, even by just a few slight acts of semiwickedness (a "little" lie, a petty theft, a kicking of one's pet), the soul tumbles into a hell where special torments are readied to fit the soul's crimes.

Zoroaster brings hell a step closer to the final judgment and damnation of Christian beliefs, but he skimps on the eternity. According to Zoroastrianism, after a world-ending apocalypse and the final triumph of Ahura Mazda, hell will be disassembled, and all souls will be able to enjoy the splendors of heaven.

BY ANY OTHER NAME

A couple of more prehell underworlds need to be mentioned before we plunge fully into hell as we know it.

The ancient Hebrew notion of the underworld was Sheol, a word possibly derived from the Assyrian word *shilu* ("chamber"). The chamber in this case referred to the physical confines of the grave—the actual hole in the ground that the dead were placed in. The word "Sheol" appears many times in the first five books of the Bible, with its meaning shifting a bit murkily between "grave" and "underworld." As an underworld, Sheol was neutral territory; all the dead went there whether they were good or wicked, rich or poor, pious or faithless. Like Duat and other underworlds before it, Sheol was a dusty, gloomy place of oblivion deep beneath the earth. It was sometimes described as the place that was the farthest possible distance from God. The dead who wandered about Sheol were not souls with active afterlives, but rather ghostly beings that existed without knowledge, memory, or feeling. They were said to be "sleepers in the dust."

The ancient Greeks circa the seventh century B.C. believed all souls headed for the underworld of Hades, a shadowy, frightening place that borrowed quite a bit of its topography from the Babylonians' Kurnugia. After making their way across the river Styx, souls wandered about in the gloom, attempting to find their way into the heaven of the Elysian fields (an equivalent to the Egyptian Field of Rushes) and hoping desperately that they were not consigned to the dark, bottomless pit of Tartarus. Hades was embraced as the underworld of the Romans as well, although on their hell maps the forbidding river to cross was the river Lethe.

The specifics and logistics of Hades—along with the full pantheon of Greek and Roman aboveground and belowground gods—faded away with the societies of ancient Greece and Rome, but the word stuck around. By the time the Hebrew scriptures were translated into Greek around the second century B.C., the word "Hades" was often substituted for "Sheol." A third term, "Gehenna," was a Greek word derived from the Hebrew term *Gehinnom*, which referred to the forbidding Valley of Hinnom south of Jerusalem. Eventually, "Gehenna" became nearly interchangeable with "Hades" and "Sheol."

By the time the Bible was being set down in English in the late fourteenth century, the two old underworlds and the desolate valley had blended into a more precise and fiery destination: hell.

PULLED DOWN

In English translations of Greek works, the souls of the dead are often referred to as "shades." A shade differs a bit from the usual notion of soul. It's not the spirit essence of a person, but rather a ghostly entity that has a physical presence in the afterlife. Shades are not capable of experiencing pleasure or pain, but they occasionally demonstrate some zombielike hunger for blood if they get their hands on a Hades-visiting mortal. Shades stumble about in the netherworlds of the *Aeneid*, the *Odyssey*, and Dante's *Inferno*, for the most part not quite sure what to do with themselves in the land of the dead. "Shade" is also sometimes used as a general synonym for "ghost," and can describe the dead of the Hebrew Sheol, the confused souls lost in the Egyptian afterlife, and spirits at the lowest point in a reincarnation cycle.

HELL IN SCRIPTURE

In the Old Testament, hell as a place is, though clearly frightening, sometimes rather sketchily defined. For the dozens of times that "Sheol" appeared in the Old Testament, it was translated alternately into English about half the time as "grave" or "pit," and about half the time as "hell." When the deceased are described as moving on to Sheol, it could sometimes be read as a rather darkly poetic statement of fact: A body was finding its final resting place in the grave (in Psalms 6:5; "For in death there is no remembrance of thee: in *the grave* who shall give thee thanks?" [italics added]). In other cases,

Sheol—translated as "hell"—carries a more ominous sense of final judgment (Later, in Psalm 9:17: "The wicked shall be turned into *hell*, and all the nations that forget God" [italics added]).

In the New Testament, the Greek word "Hades" appears, sometimes seeming to be used as a stand-in for "Sheol" and carrying the sense of "death" or "grave." But it is also used to describe a tormenting place below us, a place that is in an adversarial position to the followers of Christ. Other occurrences of "hell" are drawn from the Hebrew "Gehenna," and serve to underscore the fiery nature of the place. In the Gospel of Matthew, Jesus Christ, while delivering the Beatitudes, warns that "hell fire" will await those who give themselves over to intemperate anger and who treat others unkindly. Among the repeated references to hell in Matthew, Jesus also speaks of a "furnace of fire" in which "there shall be wailing and gnashing of teeth," and "the eternal fire, prepared for the devil and his angels."

In the New Testament's book of Revelation, hell's geography is broadened and embellished, and in a series of vivid, prophetic passages, it springs to life as an apocalyptic lake of fire, full of abominations. When Satan is imprisoned in "the bottomless pit" for a thousand-year term and then cast into that lake of fire, hell and its ruler are joined, and damned, for eternity.

RICH MAN, POOR MAN

A closer look at the way hell might function is found in Luke's Gospel, where the place is presented as a very real realm of afterlife punishment. Luke describes Jesus Christ relaying a parable in which a well-fed rich man contemptuously ignores the condition of Lazarus, a hungry beggar who resides outside the gate of the rich man's property (he's not to be confused with the Lazarus who Jesus miraculously brings back from the dead). When the rich man dies, he is stunned to find he has descended to an unnamed place of fire and torment, and he looks upward to see a sight that upsets him even more: the filthy beggar Lazarus is comfortably enfolded in the flowing robes of Abraham, father of the Judeo-Christian faith.

Suddenly, it is the rich man's turn to beg, and he pleads unsuccessfully to an unmoved Abraham for Lazarus to come down and put a spot of water on his tongue to relieve the anguish of the flames. Abraham denies the request, explaining that a gulf exists between the two of them through which nothing can now pass. The rich man begs Abraham to send the spirit of Lazarus to warn his brothers, so that they might avoid his fate.

Abraham says that if the message of Moses and the prophets hasn't been enough to warn them, they will also be unpersuaded by the sight of a beggar rising from the dead. Here, a fundamental premise of heaven and hell is made clear: A simple, faithful man who has lived a life of deprivation can rise to the bosom of Abraham, while a well-to-do man who has enjoyed the luxuries of life has no guarantee that he will see heaven. He may in fact find himself in the flames of hell. (Perhaps the most curious part of this parable is that heaven and hell are, though irrevocably separated, within shouting distance of each other. This idea—that those in heaven would be able to watch and hear the torments of those in hell—became a major theme of medieval artwork.)

MY HELL

BOB NEWHART
Actor, comic, Bob

I was thinking about hell and the "gnashing of teeth." So, I imagine everyone there would have really bad teeth. There would be a dentist—but no Novocain.

HELL BURNS

In May 2004, a fire tore through a warehouse containing the sizable and priceless modern-art collection of advertising magnate and premier art collector Charles Saatchi. Among the artwork burnt into oblivion: *Hell*, a sculpture/tableau by artists Jake and Dinos Chapman. Saatchi had reportedly paid a half million pounds to commission *Hell*, which took the artists two years to complete. Their *Hell* took the form of an enormous swastika, upon which five thousand hand-casted, hand-painted figurines of skeletons, mutants, and Nazi soldiers acted out scenes of death and destruction.

REVELATION

The final book of the Bible—alternately known as the book of Revelation, the Revelation to John, or the Revelation of Saint John the Divine—provides a spectacularly disconcerting vision of the end of the world and the final banishment of Satan into hell. The book was written toward the end of the first century, and a debate on its authorship continues. Many Christians believe that the John of Revelation is the Apostle John, who also authored the Gospel of John, while some Bible scholars believe that the Gospel and the book of Revelation have separate authors, one of whom may or may not have been the apostle.

The writing in Revelation was meant to serve as a letter to seven churches in Asia Minor, but its apocalyptic style has opened it up to various interpretations. It can be read as a literary work, in which the author indulges a rather strong penchant for elevated prose. It can be read as a historical work, in which the author, using some carefully coded language and "insider" symbolism, recounts the struggles of the early Christian church under the Roman emperors Nero and/or Domitian. But the book has often been read as a work of powerful prophecy. (And there are some different interpretations of what's being prophesied: "Preterists" hold that the book predicts events that will happen in the first century; futurists contend that all the events described in Revelation will commence shortly before the Second Coming of Christ; while the historicist approach says that the book is full of prophesies of events that have happened and will continue to happen from the first century right up through the Second Coming.)

Despite the differing points of view on how to read Revelation, there's one indisputable common point: Things are going to get extremely unpleasant. Some of Revelation's more frightening predictions are that there will be devastating earthquakes, rains of fire and blood, and a plague of ferocious locusts. A third of the world's population will die; survivors who have turned from God to worship a false prophet will be marked with painful sores; and the seas will be turned into blood. Revelation describes a "lake of fire" burning with brimstone—a crucial hell detail—and those who are thrown into the lake will suffer horribly.

Who and what get thrown in? The devil, the beast, the false prophet (the Antichrist), Death, and the pre–Judgment Day version of hell itself. As for mortals, quite a few are heading lakeward as well. Anyone whose name is not written in the Book of Life gets tossed in, along with unbelievers, abominable sinners, murderers, whoremongers, sorcerers, idolaters, and liars. There's no point in attempting to run and hide—cowards will be thrown in too.

The imagery of Revelation, particularly the lake of fire, gave hell some powerful visual substance. But at various councils and synods in the first few centuries of the Christian church, the question of whether Revelation should be considered scripture was itself a point of heated debate, with some bishops arguing against its inclusion in the New Testament on grounds that it was too confusing to laypeople. Clearly that was a losing point of view, and the text was consistently supported by such influential early church fathers as Irenaeus, Tertullian, and Clement of Alexandria. The debate was effectively ended when Revelation was recognized as part of the New Testament canon at the Third Council of Carthage in A.D. 397.

TO THE BRIM

Brimstone is actually sulfur, a common chemical element that turns up in the natural world either as free-form yellow crystals or in the form of sulfide and sulfate minerals ("sulfur" derives from an Arabic word for "yellow"). Sulfur is particularly abundant around hot springs and volcanoes; thus the English translation/nickname of "brimstone"—it's the stuff found around the brim, or rim, of craters full of bubbling hot stuff. As for that sulfurous stench—sulfur on its own is odorless, but when it teams up with hydrogen— yeesh—it reeks of rotten egg.

LOW FLIER

The United Kingdom is home to the brimstone butterfly, ostensibly named for its pale yellow wings rather than its eternal damnation.

TRACT MARKS

From the glimpses of hell available in the texts of the Bible, an entire literary genre emerged in the first centuries of the Christian church: the genre of apocalyptic literature. Works such as the Apocalypse of Paul and the Apocalypse of Peter claimed to be based on secret Gospels, lost bits of scripture, or personal writings of apostles, and they described the location and layout of hell, and the precise ways in which Judgment Day would take place. In describing hell, the authors of these texts clearly did not feel constrained by accepted scripture, and given that their setting was a place full of fallen angels, damned sinners, and bad behavior, these extra-biblical narratives could be packed with all sorts of shocking goings-on that would be deemed unseemly in any other context.

There's a good deal of bloody violence in these works, as hellish torments for particular sinners are described (blasphemers are hung up by their tongues, bad parents are ripped to shreds by demonic beasts). But often there's also a strong focus on sins that are sexual in nature, with various punishments devised for different carnal transgressions (adulterers are plunged in a river of fire, women who were not virgins when they married are flayed). The idea here may have been similar to one that has helped sneak erotica past several centuries' worth of censors: If the heated act is presented as something enjoyable, it's wicked, but if it's discussed in terms of its punishment, then it's part of an instructive, moral lesson.

HEAT FROM THE PULPIT

Hell became a blazingly prominent feature of sermons delivered in the Puritan churches of colonial America, enough so that delivering fire-and-brimstone sermons (also called "hellfire sermons") became a common, congregation-rattling method of preaching. The classic fire-and-brimstone sermon may have reached peak form in July 1741, when preacher Jonathan Edwards delivered his famously hell-centered "Sinners in the Hands of an Angry God" at a church in Enfield, Connecticut.

The sermon has been anthologized in countless American textbooks, and can be read as a piece of powerful, passionately crafted, early American literature. But Edwards's take on the nature of hell and the attitude of God toward human wickedness remains as startling and unnerving as it must have been for the congregation in Enfield. Edwards preaches that God could toss a sinful human into hell with as little thought, let alone remorse, as a human would exhibit while stepping on a worm or crushing an annoying insect. God has not the least bit of pity for sinners—he finds them to be abhorrent and abominable. A sinner asking God for mercy will only make an already wrathful God even angrier.

It is only the hand of God that keeps wicked men from immediately tumbling into the hell they deserve, and when God is provoked and angered, the hell that sinners do get dropped into is fiery, horrible, and eternal. Edwards goes to some lengths to explain just how unimaginably long an eternity is. The shrieks and cries of the sinners will be in vain—God will laugh at them.

One question that had long been raised by Christian theologians: How can anyone actually be happy in heaven if they know that some of their beloved friends and family members are roasting in hell? Edwards had an answer: Those in heaven will have the chance to look down on the "awful spectacle" of hell, and what they see will fill them with a higher level of adoration for the Lord's "great power and majesty."

Edwards's harsh interpretation of scripture eventually lost him his job. In the late 1740s, when he served as the pastor of the Congregationalist Church in Northampton, Massachusetts, Edwards pushed for stricter and stricter regulations on who could become church members and who could receive Communion. This push was not popular with his congregation or with other church leaders, and by 1750 Edwards had been asked in no uncertain terms to step down from the pulpit.

In later life he continued to write and to preach, creating a remarkable and highly influential body of work focused on the nature and meaning of Christianity. He also became involved in mission work, accepting a position with the Indian mission in Stockbridge, Massachusetts. In February 1758, he was appointed president of Princeton University (then known as the College of New Jersey), but died of complications from a smallpox inoculation just a month later.

ENDNOTE: PAIN OF SEPARATION

Perhaps we now have enough background on hell and its early incarnations to move ahead through some hotter portions of its history. But it should be understood that these days a precise definition of the nature of hell is by no means a settled matter.

On July 28, 1999, Pope John Paul II, at one of his Wednesday morning general audiences, clarified the Catholic church's position by defining hell this way: "Rather than a place, hell indicates the state of those who freely and definitively separate themselves from God, the source of all life and joy." He advised that the biblical descriptions of a hell of fire needed to be carefully interpreted, and further instructed that hell was not a punishment imposed by God, but rather a state arrived at by those who rejected God's mercy. "Damnation consists precisely in definitive separation from God, freely chosen by the human person and confirmed with death that seals his choice for ever."

This definition strongly echoed a statement made by the well-known American evangelist Billy Graham. In the November 15, 1993, issue of *Time*, Graham said, "The only thing I could say for sure is that hell means separation from God. We are separated from his light, from his fellowship. That is going to be hell. When it comes to a literal fire, I don't preach it because I'm not sure about it. When the scripture uses fire concerning hell, that is possibly an illustration of how terrible it's going to be—not fire but something worse, a thirst for God that cannot be quenched."

These statements may provide some comfort to those believers troubled by the notion of eternal fire and uneasy with the likes of Jonathan Edwards's angry God. But these points of view are far from universally embraced. In fact, both Graham and John Paul attracted harsh criticism from those who felt their statements were in effect a denial of the hell of scripture.

So, having ranged from the earliest underworlds to our modern world, the question remains: What is hell?

Perhaps the only inarguable conclusion one can reach is this: The debate burns on.

WHERE IS HELL?

*There is a high road to heaven which few people travel; hell
hath no door, but many manage to burrow their way in.*
—Chinese proverb

*Hell isn't merely paved with good intentions—it's walled
and roofed with them.* —Aldous Huxley

How does one get to hell?

Practice?

Perhaps the question should be focused a bit more
precisely: Where exactly is a soul headed when it takes
off for hell?

The easy answer is: down.

The descent motif is one of the great unifiers of hell
beliefs, and most cultures and religions have imagined
and reimagined hell to be a place way down below us,
either literally within the irritable bowels of the earth

somewhere, or in a kind of damnably abstract under-world. For the people of so many faiths, a soul heading hellward has meant a soul heading downward, and whether hell has been thought of as an excruciating circus of eternal punishment or as a calmer way station between reincarnations, it's been consistently located somewhere beneath our mortal realm.

Given that some other elements of hell have been wildly divergent from culture to culture (dusty nothingness versus lake of fire), the doggedly downward location of the place is a striking common point. But the fact that so many hells have a subterranean location is probably less a product of any shared belief than it is the reflection of a truism of human psychology—that is, we don't like the dark.

In every culture that has left behind some historical record, it is clear that the concept of light is preferable to that of darkness, and that movement upward represents some kind of gain in status, while movement downward represents a loss. It's not too hard to imagine how our distant heathen ancestors might have picked up these notions from the natural world around them. Plants and flowers sprouted upward to the sky, while grotesque little squiggly things wriggled downward into the mud. Eagles and hawks soared gloriously above, while much less glorious creatures burrowed blindly and frantically downward. The sun rose up to bring a bright new day, and sunk down to surrender to the perils of the dark night.

So it's understandable that as we humans began to puzzle out the intriguing concept of a human soul—and the transformatively powerful concept of good and evil—we would hold to the idea that a good soul rises like one of those eagles—skyward, to the sun, moon, and stars, to the heavens—while an evil soul sinks, wicked and wormlike, lower and lower into darkness and decay.

Where is hell? Perhaps the precise location is only made available on a need-to-know basis, but a brief descent may turn up some clues.

DOWN IN THE VALLEY

So much for the anthropology. Where is "real" hell? Well, it's important to begin here by noting that one of the most significant and influential points of reference for many religious conceptions of hell was, in fact, a very real piece of real estate in our own world. The hell that mortals have come to know and fear might be imagined as the most spectacularly heinous of gated communities, but some of its imagery seems to have come from a humble, unpromising tract of landfill.

Just south of ancient Jerusalem stretched an unwelcoming slash of land known as the valley of Hinnom (also referred to as the valley of Gehinnom or Ben Hinnon). Today it can still be seen as the ravine that runs west of the Old City's Jaffa Gate, continuing southeast toward the foot of Mount Zion. In ancient times, Hinnom became the focus of some geographical name-calling: It was disparagingly referred to by the prophet Jeremiah as the "valley of fire" or "valley of death," because the Canaanites who lived there had used it as a place for pagan rituals that included an unsettling mix of self-immolation, self-mutilation, and child sacrifice, all in the name of the god Moloch. "Gehinnom" became a one-word evocation of the bad, unholy side of town.

King Josiah of Judah made a concerted effort to wipe out all elements of pagan worship and, as part of this campaign, undertook the destruction of the stone altars in Hinnom upon which rites of burnt offerings and human sacrifice had once been carried out (described in 2 Kings 23).

From then on, the valley had a new purpose: It became the primary town dump for the ever-expanding Jerusalem. As such, the valley became home to swelling piles of trash, filth, and the carcasses of slaughtered animals. Thus, the valley of Hinnom was transformed from a defiled ceremonial ground into an odorous dumping ground. Subsequently, Jerusalem faced a waste management crisis as this unpopular place became the site of enough concentrated offal to become a public health risk. To prevent the spread of disease, the trash heaps of Hinnom were routinely set afire.

You might see where things are headed here—Wickedness. Carcasses. Flame.

Smell like . . . damnation?

Yes, and it gets more hellish. The valley of Hinnom had such an unpleasant function to serve and developed such an abominable reputation that it was deemed a fitting end place for the bodies of executed criminals. As a final humiliation, these bodies were also burned.

While the Jewish faith never developed a strong concept of a hell of damnation (remember Sheol?), it is easy to see how in Jewish legend and rabbinic writings this very real valley of Hinnom became a daunting symbol of fiery punishment.

It was through the process of translation that the local became the cosmological. The Hebrew word "Gehinnom" was translated into the Septuagint, the Greek bible, as "Gehenna," and "Gehenna" was eventually translated in the New Testament as "hell." "Gehenna" also served as a basis for Islamic hell, which in the Koran is translated as "Jahannam," a word now taken to mean literally "fire of hell."

Today, the valley of Hinnom no longer burns, and parts of it are lushly gardened. But it does still get at least hot enough there to pop popcorn: The area above the valley has been developed and is home to a popular movie theater, Jerusalem's Cinémathèque.

MULTIPLE POINTS OF ENTRY

- Hell's Gate National Park outside of Nairobi, Kenya
- Hells Gate State Park on the Snake River, Lewiston, Idaho, downriver from Hells Canyon
- Hell's Gate in Death Valley, California
- Hell's Gate in Gulf Savannah, Queensland, Australia
- Hell's Gate in Rotorua, New Zealand
- Hell's Gate in Saba, Netherlands Antilles
- Hell Gate, a narrow stretch of the East River, New York City

While the valley of Hinnom offers the rather rare and remarkable example of a bit of hell that began as actual, aboveground real estate, it was not the basis for all hells. In fact, in translating the word "Gehenna" to "hell," Christian theologians were indirectly referencing a very different conception of an underworld, one that was not a place of fire at all but was, to put it bluntly, frozen over.

Let's check our vocabulary here. The word "hell" derives from an Old English verb, "helan," which translates loosely as "to bury or conceal." "Helan" is in turn etymologically related to a figure from Old Norse mythology, Hel, the Viking goddess of death and the underworld.

It was the goddess's unyielding unpleasantness that got her kicked out of Asgard, the realm of the Norse gods, by Odin, the mightiest god of the bunch. Hel was sent to rule the dark and cold of Niflheim, "the house of mists," something close to a Viking Limbo. In some legends, this empty, forbidding place was a sort of holding pen for the souls of warriors who were unlucky enough not to have been slaughtered in battle. It was a place where those who had endured the horror of missing their chance at a moment of blood glory and had gone on to live long, uneventful lives could ponder their shameful lack of battlefield heroics (those who died bravely—or at least quickly—in battle went on to the Viking version of heaven, Valhalla).

As for location, even on the earthly plane, the Vikings inhabited some rather chilly and inhospitable parts of the globe, and in imagining a geography for their hell, they had to come up with something even more punishing. They believed Niflheim to be located in the unreachable northern stretches of their land, beneath the roots of Yggdrasil, the World Tree. In Norse mythology, Yggdrasil, also translated as "Odin's Horse," is the giant ash tree that links and shelters the three worlds of the gods, the living, and the dead. Niflheim was beneath the third root of the tree, at the lowest levels of the Norse universe.

Once Hel was banished there, she made her home in the lowest and most inhospitable part of Niflheim, which in tribute to its icy hostess came to be known as Helheim or Helgardh. Helheim was encircled by the formidable, raging river Gjoll, a watery boundary that made it difficult even for other gods to visit the icy realm. Then again, who wanted to drop in on Hel?

GATEWAY TO HELL: DOORWAY TO NORWAY

Just east of Trondheim, extending a greeting to fjord-bound transatlantic travelers, is the small town of Hell, Norway. In addition to offering up a decidedly non-infernoesque landscape, a Hell train station, and a variety of Honeymoon in Hell hotel specials, the town has since 1992 annually hosted the Hell Blues Festival, during which the sizable Hell Blues Choir is often a standout attraction. Music fans, draw your own conclusions: Deep Purple, Uriah Heep, and Status Quo have all been headliners in Hell.

MY HELL

MATT STONE
Writer/producer, *South Park*

I think it's fairly obvious that Hollywood is a gateway to hell. When you begin working in Hollywood, I think you have to approach it as a basic battle of good versus evil, with you being good and everyone else being evil. And

> you put up a good fight at first, trying to hang
> on to your principles and trying to do good
> work. But when you suddenly find yourself
> making warm, friendly chitchat with a Botoxed
> former soap opera star at a hundred-thousand-
> dollar bar mitzvah, you know that you have
> stepped into hell.

REALITY CHECK

As with almost every other element of hell's makeup, when it comes to the concept of hell as a place, a tricky split perspective comes into play. For centuries, religions and believers have wrestled with the question of whether hell should be considered as a "real" place with an actual presence somewhere in the physical world, as a real place that exists somehow outside the physical universe, or as a kind of spiritual metaphor. There have been a boggling variety of councils convened, decrees issued, churches split, and wars waged over this question, and debate continues to this day. It's important to remember that in the ancient world, in prescientific times, when an individual's experience of the world might be limited to a few miles of earth and a few score of people, this question did not really have to be answered conclusively one way or the other.

For the Vikings, who no doubt struggled to make sense of so much of the harsh natural world around them, the realms of Valhalla and Helheim and the pantheon of gods could be embraced as both truth and story. The idea of a great three-rooted tree that holds the universe together may seem to modern minds silly if not easily disprovable, but the power of the myth brought an order and substance to the Vikings' view of their world. The weight of belief behind the story made it, in essence, the truth.

And that ability to have it both ways—to at once consider hell as a real, mapped place and a work of imagination—is something that will be encountered again and again in different eras and cultures.

HOT NEIGHBORHOOD

The area of Manhattan west of Eighth Avenue, between Thirty-fourth and Fifty-ninth Streets, has long been referred to as Hell's Kitchen. No one is quite sure where the name came from, though the neighborhood was the site of fierce gang wars in the nineteenth century and was home to many slaughterhouses and arson-plagued stretches of tenements. Developers in the 1950s and 1960s tried to erase any hint of damnation by calling the neighborhood Clinton after the area's association with former New York governor De Witt Clinton, but many residents have remained resolutely proud of being a part of Hell's Kitchen. These days real estate agents seem intent on cursing the area once more with the damnably generic "Midtown West."

BIG FAT GREEK (AND ROMAN) HELL

The reign of the Greek and Roman gods of Mount Olympus lasted over a thousand years, up until the fifth century A.D. At least one reason they were able to rule as long as they did was that these gods not only functioned as figures of worship but also as figures of art, literature, and pop culture. The exploits of Zeus, Hera, Hades, and the like offered up exactly the same kind of zippy satisfaction that modern audiences derive from following the exploits of loved and loathed celebrities. That's exactly why we know so much about the hell of both the Greeks and the Romans: The places were brought to life in meticulous detail through works of phenomenal storytelling intended for the entertainment and edification of general audiences of the day.

Homer and Hesiod were both epic poets of eighth-century B.C. Greece whose storytelling abilities were widely celebrated. The classical Greek vision of hell—called Hades—that emerges from the work of these two makes the Greek underworld a place both real and fantastic.

While Hesiod is much less familiar to modern readers than Homer, he formalized some of the crucial details of the Greek hell in his principal work, *Theogony.* Hesiod describes a Hades surrounded by the river Styx and guarded by a frighteningly distemperate hellhound, Cerberus. And as if Hades were not hellish enough, Hesiod also describes a kind of hell's hell: the despicable and mortifying Pit of Tartarus, which lies beneath Hades. Homer's *Odyssey* contains one of the seminal journeys to the underworld, and it's sometimes easy to forget that the intention behind this storytelling was to create a goose bump–inducing narrative, not a work of religious catechism or a dry recounting of historical fact. In the *Odyssey*, Odysseus struggles mightily, confronting clingy nymphs, singing Sirens, and a hungry Cyclops before he finds the entrance to Hades just a few feet beneath the surface of the earth, within a cave in a remote region of the southern Peloponnese.

And while some of the underworldly goings-on in Hades may have been recognized as the work of poets, the place itself was understood to be a real chunk of geography, with the remote, mysterious cave that held its entrance turning up on Greek nautical maps. That no mortal seemed to be able to follow those maps well enough to actually sail to the place for a visit simply added to its dark mystique.

ALL ABOARD

Some of the earliest writings on the final destination of the soul come from ancient Babylon, capital city of the Middle Eastern land of Babylonia in Mesopotamia. Today, the town of Babylon is the final destination for thousands of eastbound souls riding the Babylon line of New York's Long Island Rail Road. Coincidence? Yes, obviously.

PIT OF PITS

For the nastiest of mortal behavior, the Greeks did not consider Hades to be the worst afterlife environment one might have to endure. That dishonor went to the infinitely darker and scarier Tartarus, a forbidding bottomless pit that was even lower than Hades. While the plain old dead wandered through Hades, Greeks who committed the most heinous sins (killing a parent à la Oedipus) could expect to find themselves stuck in the inescapable pit— down so low that Hades looked like up to them.

HELL OF A SHOW

In September 2003, Hell on Earth, a Saint Petersburg, Florida-based heavy metal band made some national rock 'n' roll news by announcing that at an upcoming Saturday night show, a terminally ill person would commit suicide onstage, ostensibly to call attention to the right-to-die movement. When word of the suicide show spread, the Saint Petersburg City Council quickly passed an ordinance forbidding suicide

70

committed for commercial or entertainment purposes. A Florida judge issued a temporary injunction forbidding the "suicide show" from taking place within Saint Petersburg city limits. After losing its scheduled club booking due to the uproar, Hell on Earth, undeterred, announced that the show would take place anyway, at an undisclosed location, and that the suicide would be broadcast "live" over the Internet.

The buildup to the show was covered extensively by media ranging from the Associated Press to CNN to *Rolling Stone*. But it's unclear whether the suicide or the show ever happened. According to the *St. Petersburg Times*, the band's Web site crashed shortly before the scheduled performance was to take place.

BRINGING HELL HOME

"We want you—and your Hades." It's hard to imagine wanting to claim hell for one's own as a matter of military conquest, but that's what happened as the Hellenistic civilization of ancient Greece gave way to the spread of the

Roman Empire. The Romans had developed their own religious beliefs, a kind of naturalistic pantheism, but perhaps in the spirit of "to the victors, the spoils," they recognized something powerful and desirable in the grand mythology of the Greeks. So, as the empire spread, Greek myths were appropriated along with the territory. In essence, the Romans conquered the Greeks' hell and made it their own.

The first-century B.C. poet Virgil provided the most detailed descriptions of Roman hell in his epic work, the *Aeneid.* In this work, the easily mispronounced Aeneas, a Trojan warrior on an *Odyssey*-like series of adventures, also has to cross a river Styx and sneak past a hound of hell to get a peek at the Roman underworld. But there is a crucial difference to the place: Hell has been moved to give it home-court advantage. Virgil, along with many other Roman poets, moved hell from its Peloponnesian location and brought it to local turf, locating its gateway in a cave on the shore of Lake Avernus, just outside modern-day Naples.

GETTING BENT

The term "hell-bent," meaning "recklessly determined," has been in use since 1835.

The hellbender is a giant North American sala-

> mander that is neither particularly reckless nor
> determined. But its skin can secrete toxic slime.

SKEPTICAL

Roman times also offer a new twist to the "Where is
hell?" question: the voice of the dismissive and disgusted
skeptic. The poet and philosopher Lucretius lived in the
first century B.C., and his major work, *On the Nature of
Things*, carefully and methodically laid out a radical idea:
Humanity is simply and inextricably a part of the natural
world, and there are no grand afterworlds that spirits
ascend or descend to. In fact, Lucretius considered any
discussion of the nature or location of hell to be a foolish
waste of mortal breath. And he believed that all the talk
of Hades pointed up the two biggest reasons people were
unable to enjoy their lifetimes on earth: fear of the gods
and fear of death.

Lucretius was a proponent of Epicureanism (from
the fourth-century B.C. philosopher Epicurus), a world-
view that prized the experience of pleasure, peace of
mind, and freedom from fear, and frowned upon the
baser concerns of the roiling, smaller-scale matters of

politics. With *On the Nature of Things,* Lucretius offers up some strikingly ahead-of-his-time thoughts on such topics as psychology, evolution, and even atomic theory, but his theological points of view stand out. He believed that most human minds were held in a kind of slavery to their fears and superstitions, and that Roman priests exploited these fears to build up their own authority. He conceded that there were gods, but that those entities were not concerned with the day-to-day lives of humans. And he dismissed the tales of famously punished sinners such as Sisyphus and Tantalus as stories created by the fearful living rather than as glimpses of afterlife realities.

It's probably not a surprise that Lucretius's view was not very popular. He is not discussed or credited in the works of other major poets, and is barely mentioned in the works of early Christian writers (some historians have suggested that because of his antireligious slant, there was a concerted effort to ignore Lucretius). The one time he is memorably mentioned in another's writing, it's for a put-down. Jerome, an influential fourth-century A.D. Christian scholar credited with translating the Hebrew and Greek versions of the Bible into Latin, claimed that Lucretius had driven himself crazy by drinking a powerful love potion, and that his easily dismissible writings were scribbled down between bouts of utter insanity.

SWAHILI REMIX

In the seventh and eighth centuries A.D., as traveling Muslim merchants from Arab countries established trade with the east African coast, beliefs that had grown from those early fires of Gehenna took hold there and blended with indigenous concepts of an afterlife. The Swahili vision of hell became a prime example of this kind of heated cultural cross-pollination.

Swahili, which literally means "coast," referred to the people, culture, and language of the stretch of east African coast including Somalia, Kenya, Tanzania, and Mozambique. The Swahili language itself was essentially the African Bantu language with an Arabic influence.

Damnationwise, in the resulting blend of Muslim monotheism and Swahili animism, the entrance to hell was located just a little farther than any man could walk in a day (i.e., it was a real place on earth, but a mortal could never quite get there to investigate it). In keeping with the descent motif of other cultures, this hell—"kuzimu" in Swahili parlance—took the form of an elaborate sub-terranean structure that reached deep below the surface of the earth, which, in its maze-like construction and ever-shifting protocols, seemed to be set up like a kind of ultimately horrific DMV. It was believed that this hell was the seventh element of the universe that God created, and so it descended accordingly through seven different levels: the worse the soul of the condemned, the lower the level it was assigned to. And while it's unlikely that Viking seamen and Swahili tribesmen ever sat around exchanging theories of damnation, the worst of Swahili hell, like the Norse hell, was a place without fire. It was believed that the worst sinners—atheists, water thieves, and other souls beyond any hope of redemption—spent eternity in a hell of bone-chilling cold.

YOU DIRTY RAT

For some Hindu believers, a passage through and around the hells of the afterlife is all part of the cycle of life, and the actual punishment for an unvirtuous soul takes the form of a particularly ugly reincarnation. As human existence is at the top level of the earthly plane for a soul, any step into another form of life is a step away from enlightenment. But while some souls might not particularly mind an earthly go-round as an eagle, an elk, a fox, or even a boar, those who find themselves reborn as lesser creatures—rats, worms, insects—have no choice but to accept that they are being punished. The only upside is that an earthly lifetime of rodenthood or sliminess is considered sufficient punishment for whatever a soul's transgressions happened to be. If a soul learns its lesson and lives well, even as a rat, next time around the soul can step up to a better life.

NEW-WORLD HELLS

The Aztec civilization developed a hell in which time was a more predominant concern than was place. Their hell, Mictlan, was loosely understood to be an underworld, but more importantly it was across another one of those forbidding rivers, and the real punishment of the afterlife was in the long journey it took to get to Mictlan. As with the Egyptian and Tibetan Books of the Dead, the Aztecs had a system of prayers and spirit advice that the living could offer to departed souls to help them on their journeys.

Mayans believed in a nine-leveled underworld that was known collectively as Xibalba. Each level was ruled by its own lord of death, and hell was found at the lowest level of Xibalba in a place called Mitnal. Mitnal was ruled by a death god with the punchy name of Ah Puch, and was somewhat akin to the Greeks' Tartarus—it was the lowest of low places. But those in the rest of Xibalba didn't have it easy. According to the Mayan text the Popol Vuh, the whole of the underworld was unremittingly unpleasant, a fact made clear by the names of some of the strange entities who inhabited it. The ever abominable Ah Puch was assisted by a hell staff that included such lords of death as Stab Master, Bone Scepter, Skull Scepter, Pus Master, and Blood Gatherer.

HARROWING

Hell's descent motif was emphasized in a bit of extra-biblical Christian text, the Apostles' Creed. The creed's name may be something of a misnomer. Early traditional beliefs maintained that it was written by the original apostles ten days after Jesus's ascension into heaven. However, many scholars now believe it was developed over the first couple of centuries of the church, for use as a cogent summary of Christian doctrine to be recited by baptismal candidates. In describing what happened to Jesus between Good Friday and Easter Sunday, the creed traditionally says that "he descended into hell; the third day he rose again from the dead; he ascended into Heaven, and sitteth at the right hand of God the Father Almighty."

The idea of Jesus traveling to hell has been controversial, and some Christian denominations leave out that part of the creed. But early interpretations of Jesus's descent and descriptions of what he did while he was there turned up in such early apocryphal writings as the Gospel of Bartholomew and the Gospel of Nicodemus. In accounts of the Harrowing ("harrowing" meaning "to pillage or plunder"), Jesus is not just passively waiting for the moment of his resurrection but is actively battling Satan and conquering hell. In doing so, he frees Abraham, Issac, and the other patriarchs of the church, along with ancient souls such as Adam, Eve, and Noah, and allows those who died before the time of Christ to ascend to Christian heaven.

The Harrowing stories were popular, but they raised some difficult theological questions. If Satan had already been defeated by Christ, why was there still rampant evil in the world? And if hell had been shut down and the souls within freed, what precisely was going to happen on Judgment Day?

FIELD TRIPS

In the first few centuries of the Christian church, works such as the Apocalypse of Peter and the Apocalypse of Paul used prominent Bible characters to provide first-hand accounts of the Apocalypse. During medieval times, a second wave of literary accounts of travels to hell began to grow. Throughout Europe, there appeared a variety of tales of ordinary men and women taking extraordinary journeys to hell and back. Like the previous apocalyptic tracts, these stories were often strictly formatted. The usual logline: A protagonist suffers a grave illness, falls into a coma, or approaches imminent death through what should have been preventable circumstances (often the person inadvertently eats something poisonous). The protagonist's soul steps out of his or her body, and is greeted by an angel. The angel says that the protagonist can return to live the rest of his or her life, but first the angel wants to show the person what awaits in hell if the protagonist does not begin living a better life. The journey begins.

Hell in these stories is a part of the natural world and is easy to get to with an angel's guidance. The protagonists are usually led through a physical world that is familiar to them, but that now reveals strange additions: Over a town's river there is a bridge where there was none before; at the edge of town is a steep valley the protagonist has never seen before.

The Venerable Bede, a seventh-century English monk, collected some of these visions of hell in his massive work, *Ecclesiastical History of the English People.* One of the most striking accounts of a hell visit, from a monk named Drythelm, is not presented as a tale but as an actual account of what turned this brother toward his life of piety.

Drythelm is living the life of an ordinary English family man when one day he suddenly drops dead at home. The next morning, he greatly startles his family by springing back to life, after which he quickly splits up his possessions among family members and announces that he is off to spend the rest of his life in a monastery.

The family is left shocked and stunned, but we readers learn that while Drythelm was dead, he was led by an angel "of shining countenance and bright apparel" to the edge of his town, where he encountered a massive, mysterious valley he had not seen before. As flames can be seen bursting forth from one end of the valley, Drythelm assumes that the valley itself is hell, but the angel tells him he hasn't seen true damnation yet. The angel leads the puzzled Drythelm to a distant region of the valley, through a land of utter darkness, where finally they come upon a stinking, flaming pit, into which hideous, evil demons are dragging a variety of condemned souls. Drythelm recognizes a clergyman, a town citizen, and a woman of ill repute just before they vanish into the pit's darkness. The demons rush at Drythelm, but the angel fends them off. The angel doesn't need to say much more for his guest to get the point: If Drythelm doesn't turn his life in a more pious direction, he will find himself back in this valley, with no one to stop him from being dragged into the pit.

So, with the dream ended, he rockets up out of his deathbed, distributes his stuff to his dumbfounded family, and zooms away for a life of prayerful repentance. Drythelm will spend his second chance at life thanking the Lord that he got a second chance.

PERSONAL DAYS

Some vision literature didn't make the journey all the way to hell, but still managed to reveal some interesting details about the place. *The Voyage of Saint Brendan* recounts the wild, seafaring adventures of the saint, and is in the tradition of "imramha," Celtic adventure stories that are somewhat equivalent to the *Odyssey* or the *Aeneid*. The historical Saint Brendan was a sixth-century Irish monk who did indeed sail widely through the British Isles, and who founded a number of abbeys and monasteries, including a highly prominent one at Clonfert in County Galway. *The Voyage of Saint Brendan* was probably first penned in the eleventh century and became such a widely popular work that scores of versions in a number of languages have since turned up.

In *The Voyage of Saint Brendan*, a band of hardy monks set off with their leader in a specially constructed boat with the purpose of exploring mysterious regions of the wide open ocean and, perhaps, the Promised Land. What ensues is a seven-year voyage during which Brendan and crew encounter sea monsters, strange islands, and a host of beautiful white birds that turn out to be the souls of fallen angels (Brendan learns this from the birds themselves, who are still capable of normal speech). The trip takes an ominous turn when the boat comes up against a frightening chunk of smoking mountain rising up out of the sea. From the demons attempting to pelt his ship with fire and rocks, Brendan deduces precisely where he has sailed to: the edge of hell.

A short distance away, the sailors come across

perhaps the most remarkable sight of the whole voyage. Sitting on a small lump of rock in the middle of the sea is a damp and lonely Judas Iscariot, betrayer of Christ. When Brendan asks Judas what he is doing out there, Judas explains that although he has been condemned to hell and is horribly tormented by demons six days a week, a merciful Christ has allowed that every Sunday he be allowed to take a day off from damnation and sit on the rock. Judas says he is also permitted a short, wet vacation on the rock for Christmas and Easter.

Judas begs Brendan to put in a good word for him and get him an extra day on the rock before he has to return to hell. Brendan does so, and Judas receives twenty-four extra hours of rock time, although a band of screaming demons makes it clear that they are not very happy about this.

COLD DAYS IN HELL

Hell, Michigan, is an unincorporated community located about twenty miles northwest of Ann Arbor. The former swampland that Hell sits on was once home to the Potawatomi tribe, but became home to white settlers in the 1830s.

Legend has it that when town founder George Reeves, a mill owner and whiskey maker, was asked what he wanted to call the new burg, he replied, "I don't care. You can name it Hell if you want to." Legend also suggests that when Reeves later thought better of his response and tried to change the town's name to Reevesville or Reeve's Mills, he was rebuffed. These days, Hell makes a big deal out of Halloween, with a number of events, including a 10K run through Hell. And every April 15th, there's a small party at the Hell Post Office (located within the Hell Country Store and Spirits), where taxpayers can enjoy the thrill of having their returns postmarked from Hell.

BY POPULAR VOTIVE

In 1995, artist David Glenn Rinehart designed *Go to Hell*, an installation piece for the Gallery of Modern Art in Glasgow. For the piece, plywood effigies of two public figures were to be hung by a pole that would have them suspended and perfectly balanced over the gallery floor. Museum visitors would pay a pound to purchase a candle, which a tuxedo-clad attendant would affix to the effigy of their choice. The weight of the candle would lower an effigy closer to the floor than its partner; at five each afternoon, the effigy weighted with more candles and closer to the floor—and thereby closer to hell—would represent the figure that the public had voted to send to hell. Both effigies would then be doused in gasoline and burned on museum grounds. The public could then vote in person or over the Internet to choose the next set of public figures to candle it out.

The work did not get past the conceptual phase. According to Rinehart, "The closest I got to implementing it was when one curator said, 'You're not really serious are you?'"

MEMBERS ONLY

Not everyone has wanted to put off a descent to hell as long as possible. In the eighteenth century, several groups of prominent English aristocrats decided to embrace their fate as damned souls and enjoy themselves while they could: They started the hard-partying, nudity-encouraged, semisatanic gentleman's associations that came to be known as hellfire clubs.

The nature and membership of such clubs have remained understandably shrouded in secrecy, but apparently for a large number of wealthy, male, self-respecting sinners, membership in a hellfire club was a mark of pleasure-hunting VIP distinction. Then again, the purported history of hellfire clubs has been surrounded by so much sensational rumor and outsize legend that it's hard to know how much "hell" there really was within these clubs.

A phenomenal amount of legend has come to surround one club, started by Sir Francis Dashwood (1708–1781), a wealthy heir who, after a youth spent carousing about Europe, went on to a distinguished career as a member of Parliament, chancellor of the exchequer, and postmaster general. Through his early travels, Dashwood apparently picked up some interest in paganism and the occult, as well as a rather pronounced antipathy toward Christianity. So, sometime in the 1740s, he began to gather around him a group of like-minded high achievers for the purpose of poking fun at the issues of the day, mocking religious customs, and drinking to excess. In honor of their organizer, the group members began to refer to themselves as Franciscans (they never actually referred to their group as a hellfire club). They held their meetings either at favorite pubs or at Dashwood's home, but eventually Dashwood sought a proper clubhouse for his spirited brethren and leased the former Medmenham Abbey, near his family's estate in West Wycombe, for use as a party headquarters.

A few of Dashwood's renovations to the abbey hinted at sinful goings-on within: A Rabelaisian motto carved above the front door read *Fay ce que vouldras* ("Do as thou will"); the gardens around the place were groomed into various displays of botanical eroticism; and statuary were put up in some unmistakably rude poses. The abbey's library was stocked with the best of bawdy, ribald, and racy works, and also seems to have included a shockingly extensive collection of erotica. Anyone entering the abbey's dining hall couldn't miss a prominent statue of Harpocrates, the Greek god of silence and secrecy, whose message must have been clear: "What happens at the abbey stays at the abbey."

But what exactly happened at the abbey? It's quite possible that the statues and the shrubbery were about as erotic as things got around Dashwood's grounds, and it's possible—maybe even more than likely—that meetings there were nothing more than some well-heeled friends getting together for brandy, off-color stories, and male bonding. However, legend (and perhaps some dark wishful thinking) has portrayed Dashwood and his "Mad Monks of Medmenham" as fully debauched satanists, partial to Black Masses and wild orgies. Almost immediately after meetings at Medmenham commenced, stories began to circulate about the terrible things happening at the old abbey—that local girls were ritually deflowered there during hellfire gatherings, or that prostitutes hired for the evening and slyly referred to as Franciscan "nuns" were made to commit unspeakable acts of blasphemy and depraved carnality. Such rumors seem to have been started by political enemies of Dashwood and former Franciscans who had fallen out of favor with the group, and were gleefully pounced upon by gossip-mongers. And it was through that gossiping that Dashwood's bunch became a "hellfire club."

Hellfire club stories got darker and wilder after Dashwood renovated a labyrinth of caves that ran beneath his family mansion in West Wycombe. Again, there were some outside hints that the caves might be used for more than just some amateur spelunking—a statue of the Roman goddess of love, Venus, stood on a small hill above a cavern entrance that was made to look distinctly vaginal. But did Dashwood and friends don black robes in the privacy of the caves for nights of rowdy devil-worshipping and rampant fornication?

Probably not, but the legend flourished anyway.

Whatever may have gone on in the abbey and the caves, Dashwood's partying brotherhood eventually fell apart due to nothing more sensational than old age. And, in his later years, Dashwood took on a project that doesn't fit very well with his devilish reputation: He assisted one Benjamin Franklin in rewriting a version of the Church of England's Book of Common Prayer.

Oddly enough, the hellfire clubs of legend have spawned some very real hellfire clubs today: The name is frequently used by organizations catering to fans of sexual fetishism.

HELL ON A HILL

A hellfire club was started in the 1730s by an Irish earl, with that club using a hunting lodge in the hills overlooking Dublin. That massive, stone Hell-Fire Club building still stands, and while original club meetings may have been similar to Dashwood's—drink and talk rather than sex and blasphemy—through the years the place has built up its own hellish lore of hauntings, occult rituals, and satanic visitations.

TO HELL IN A TRAM

In the High Country region of British Columbia, the rushing waters of the Fraser River find themselves eventually constrained by a narrow, rocky bottleneck in the form of a glacially carved, one-hundred-foot-wide gorge. This is Hell's Gate, so named by intrepid explorer and fur trader Simon Fraser, who summed up his gorge-bound expedition of 1808 by proclaiming, "We had to travel where no human being should venture—for surely we have encountered the gates of hell." Peering into this Hell's Gate today, observers don't get a view of tormented souls at the end of a wicked life, but they can watch toiling salmon at the end of a spawning run. Visitors can casually cross Hell's Gate by way of a pedestrian bridge, or can take to heavenly heights by way of an Airtram strung across the gorge. After the tram ride, visitors can consume the watery souls who have given up their toil at the Salmon House restaurant.

Today, Christian beliefs still range from the idea that hell is a very real physical place to the idea that hell is strictly metaphorical, and back to the middle-ground stance that hell is real but exists in some spiritual dimension outside our physical world.

For some believers, centuries of scientific inquiry and advancement have not been seen to conclusively dismiss the notion of a literal hell. Instead, some find that science can be embraced to prove conclusively that there is a literal hell, which can be found at the center of the earth.

Some have found support for such a position by comparing one of Christ's descriptions of hell with recent advances in deep-sea oceanography. In the mid-1970s, some previously inaccessible parts of the Pacific Ocean floor were explored, and one of the most surprising discoveries was that of hydrothermal vents. A mile beneath the sea, in places where the earth's crust was at its thinnest, scientists observed the phenomenon of super-heated water—sometimes as hot as seven hundred degrees Fahrenheit—shooting up out of the crust (the water never actually boiled because of the extreme pressure of the deep-sea environment). Such hydrothermal vents have since been found in the Atlantic, Arctic, and Indian oceans as well.

At first it was thought that no forms of life could possibly exist near these vents, particularly since the heated water contained a toxic brew of hydrogen sulfide gas. But further investigation revealed a strange surprise: Clustered around many of the vents were a strange species of gigantic tube worm, sometimes reaching eight feet in length, that could not only withstand the extreme temperature, but could also survive by absorbing the sulfur (brimstone, that is) from the gas and converting it to nutrients. These creatures have been extremely puzzling to many scientists, but an explanation can be found in scripture. In Mark 9:48, Jesus refers to hell as a place "where their worm dieth not, and the fire is not quenched."

NOISY HELLHOLE

If hell is in fact located within the center of the earth, wouldn't all of our mining and digging of the planet have produced some other evidence of the place? There are those who believe that this evidence exists.

According to a widely spread, modern hell legend, a group of geologists overseeing a massive drilling project in Siberia attempted to drill farther into the earth than had ever been accomplished, using a drill equipped with ultrasensitive microphones and thermometers. When they had drilled about nine miles into the crust of the earth, the team made some remarkable discoveries. The drill began to spin wildly as if it were encountering no resistance, indicating that the core of the earth was hollow. The temperatures at that depth reached over two thousand degrees Fahrenheit, much higher than had been expected. And after some futzing with the microphone setup, the team heard a sound that absolutely terrified them: the sound of thousands, perhaps millions, of humans screaming in pain. In short, the team had drilled its way to hell. The expedition and its shocking discovery were reported to a respected Finnish science journal, *Ammennusastia*.

One might assume this to be pretty big news, the kind that might attract considerable interest from the UN, or at least CNN. But the story seems to have been most widely circulated in 1989 by televangelists based in Southern California.

As the story spread, it attracted believers, but it also drew a number of debunkers, among whom were a great number of devout Christians. One who did exceptional work in getting the truth behind the story was author and broadcaster Rich Buhler, whose TruthOrFiction.com specializes in unraveling rumors and urban legends. Buhler's investigation revealed that *Ammennusastia* was not a respected science journal but rather a small, monthly newsletter put out by Finnish Christians. They'd run the story based on the recollections of a staff member who had read it in a small newspaper, which in turn had run the story as part of a letter from a reader. Buhler traced the story through its appearances in newsletters and other publications, concluding that the drilling-to-hell tale had one of the classic elements of an urban legend: Publications had quoted each other's sensational bits of pseudo-information until those tidbits picked up the weight of stone fact.

Two final twists of the hellhole drill: First, the story still has life; it seems that as with most urban legends, almost every effort to carefully debunk it also serves as a means for spreading it as a reporting of fact. And second, if you dig around on the Internet, you can find audio files of those screams from hell, just as they were heard by the questionably existent Siberian drill team. Apparently, hell sounds a lot like a bad Halloween party at a sports bar.

NOT HARD TO GET TO

According to the Bhagavad Gita, a sacred text of Hinduism, hell is accessible—perhaps a little too accessible—to all mortals. Chapter 16 of the work teaches that "lust, anger and greed are the three gates of hell." If you can give up these three, you can attain a place in paradise. But if you give in to any of them, you've got no chance at either perfection or happiness.

BAD TRIP

Some modern minds would contend that to get to hell, one does not have to travel downward. Instead, one merely needs to get a spiritual toe across the line separating life and death.

In 1975, Raymond Moody, a medical doctor and parapsychologist, published a seminal work on the phenomenon of near-death experiences, *Life after Life*. Moody described the experiences of a variety of people who suffered clinical death and were then resuscitated, often with powerful memories of what their soul or spirit had experienced while their physical body was lifeless. Many of Moody's subjects reported feelings of peacefulness; visions of white, warm light; and groups of welcoming deceased relatives. But others who have been through a near-death experience (NDE) seem to have gotten a glimpse of something more forbidding.

There is a substantial group of accounts by those who have "died" on operating tables and then been resuscitated that sound very much like quick excursions to hell, a phenomenon focused on in works such as Maurice S. Rawlings's *To Hell and Back*. Individuals find themselves rushing through a blazing tunnel toward a lake of fire, or subjected to impenetrable darkness and heat of blast-furnace intensity, or sinking through a fiery rain; then they suddenly find themselves back in their bodies, usually surrounded by some startled "We thought you were a goner" medical personnel. In fact, hell-bound near-death experiences seem to cover a wide range of netherworlds: There are lakes of fire, fires on mountains, fires in deserts, and sometimes no fire at all, just icy oppressive darkness. "Angels of death" and dark, mysterious messengers are also commonly encountered, but no one seems to catch sight of an actual Satan or any other gods of hell (perhaps they don't reveal themselves until you are fully checked in).

As the personal experiences of the near dead do not often mesh particularly well with religious doctrines, NDEs have become somewhat controversial among faithful, traditional believers. Some of them offer an alternative explanation of NDEs: Satan himself creates the illusion of such experiences in order to cast doubt on the teachings of the church.

MY HELL

GEORGE DALZELL
Author, medium

I've had the opportunity to consult with some of the most gifted mediums in the world, and I've participated in science experiments, serving as a sitter and a medium. I've witnessed outrageous phenomena firsthand through the physical mediumship of the Scole Group. I was raised in a fundamentalist Christian household, and I've always believed that if anyone survived death, it could be proven by science—that simple. I participated in a mediumship experiment called White Crow on December 17, 2000, and after that I was convinced beyond doubt that there is an afterlife. But afterlife appears to be a part of our natural progression, and nobody is excluded from growing and learning. So I've seen heaven, but I've seen no evidence of the traditional version of afterlife called hell. If I did, I would truthfully admit it. What I have observed is that even people who lack conscience wind up punishing themselves for their misdeeds. We are our own worst enemy.

SUNNING WITH THE DEVIL

On the otherwise paradisiacal vacation destination of Grand Cayman Island, Hell is a very real place, though religious faith has nothing to do with its existence. The very small town of Hell—so named for the jagged black rock formations of its coast—couldn't be happier with the tourist trade its moniker has encouraged. Visitors make use of the tiny post office, painted inferno red, for the opportunity to have their postcards postmarked from Hell. A town greeter frequently turns up in satanic garb, and a few local vendors make sure that Hell tourists can remember their trip with all manner of devilish memorabilia and hellishly tacky souvenirs.

NOT IN KANSAS

The spooky allure of a potential gateway to hell can still be a powerful draw. In the 1970s, the tiny town of Stull, Kansas, ten miles west of the city of Lawrence, became the center of a bit of hellish folklore. Through a mix of ghost-story gossip and some tenuously researched college newspaper articles, a story began to circulate that Stull Cemetery and its adjacent abandoned, decaying limestone church contained one of the seven gateways to hell. (Some interpretations of the book of Revelation claim that these gateways would be revealed to all when the book's seventh seal is opened, ushering in the Apocalypse.) The Stull legend did not deign to reveal where the other six gateways might be, but it was sometimes posited that the Stull Cemetery was chosen by the devil because it was close to the precise geographical center of the United States.

The growing legend held that sometime in the mid-1800s, when the town was just being settled, Satan had impregnated a Stull woman, who delivered a stillborn, misshapen, half-human, half-demon creature that was laid to rest in Stull Cemetery. It was said that every Halloween at the stroke of midnight the devil would climb up a hidden stone stairway in the abandoned church and appear briefly to pay his respects to his dead child. The cemetery was also said to be the scene of many unexplainable and diabolical phenomenon: strange, localized winds; rain that fell around the roofless church but never inside it; and cemetery visitors who felt they were being grabbed by spirit hands.

The stories were backed with flimsy evidence at best, but they began to take hold strongly. Halloweens began to bring crowds to the cemetery to wait for the devil's visitation, even though the dark lord seems to have been a consistently uncooperative no-show. Crowds eventually became so large and unruly that, by the late 1980s, the Douglas County sheriff's department had to have a special patrol of the area on Halloween, with tickets for criminal trespass given to anyone caught on the privately owned property. Eventually, Stull residents and the property owners grew so irritated with vandals and trespassers wreaking havoc in the cemetery that security fences were installed and the grounds were patrolled nightly.

The Stull stairway to hell was never found, or at least it was never used by the devil. And it's now even more unlikely that the devil will make an appearance in Stull. According to the *Lawrence Journal-World*, the remnants of the old stone church were torn down on March 29, 2002. If the devil ever does visit, he'll have to make do with one of the reservable campsites at nearby Clinton State Park.

ENDNOTE: YOU CAN GET THERE FROM HERE

As is the case with any prime piece of real estate, hell has often depended upon location, location, location, and that location has most often been beneath us. With that matter of geography settled, we can move ahead to a closer look at what's going on within the premises. But here is a final twist of hell placement to consider: the earth itself as hell.

The Gnostic Cathars of twelfth-century France believed that God and heaven were in a spirit realm, while Satan oversaw all of the material world. So humans were essentially born into hell, in the grips of the devil from Day One. A human soul, through some strenuously ascetic living (poverty, celibacy, veganism), might eventually achieve a oneness with the spirit realm and, after death, rise to the perfection of heaven, but there was no punishment worse than life on earth.

Since hell was right here and not part of the hereafter, a doomed soul did not die and go someplace harder, hotter, and more awful than earth. Instead, the doomed soul was condemned to trudge through another round of the same damned life it was used to.

WHAT GOES ON?

That thing of hell and eternal punishment is the most absurd, as well as the most disagreeable thought that ever entered into the head of mortal man. —George Berkeley

If we had more hell in the pulpit, we would have less hell in the pew.
—Billy Graham

Damnation. Eternal punishment. Separation from God.

These are big ideas, and certainly frightening enough on their own.

But it also seems that clerics, prophets, writers, philosophers, and believers-in-general have found these basic statements of hell's purpose to be, at times, a bit too general. As many of the more neutral land-of-the-dead underworlds gave way to the fiery concept of a final judgment based on individual morality, there was (and continues to be) a great deal of debate as to how a place like hell actually functioned.

Knowing that hell is there and knowing that it is for the wicked and the unsaved is, certainly, a simple enough concept. But who exactly are the wicked? What differentiates the saved from the unsaved? What sins and crimes committed by the living are a sure path to damnation, and what errant, I'm-so-sorry-I-did-that actions can be atoned for?

The damnable fate of thieves and murderers has always been an easy call, but for at least a couple of millennia there have been catalogs of lesser sins that, if not quite sealing the deal, got the soul headed in a hellward direction. In Western beliefs, these lists achieved semi-official form as the seven deadly sins: pride, greed, sloth, lust, anger, gluttony, and envy. Then again, some Gnostic sects have believed it was these very sins that provided the ticket to heaven—a soul couldn't rise heavenward until it had rid itself of sinful desires by indulging in as much sin as possible.

And then there have been those who believed that a soul's rap sheet of sins was not as important as its salvation. For example, fourth-century theologian Augustine turned up the heat in hell by teaching that, no matter an individual's degree of virtue, anyone who was not both baptized as a Christian and accepting of Jesus Christ would burn in hell.

Even when the grounds for damnation have been established, there has often been debate over the precise processing a soul will be put through in hell. Are all damned souls equally abominable, or are certain, specially designed torments assigned to particular sinners? Does a soul move through hell in some way, or is it fixed in a singular permanent state of damnation? And are there any infernal loopholes in the system that might allow for a soul to escape from hell?

How exactly does hell work?

While mortals have an understandably limited perspective on the place, that clearly hasn't stopped them from offering some detailed points of view.

GOING GREEK

Of all the ancient Greek philosophers, the reigning heavyweights are Socrates, Plato, and Aristotle. The three form an interesting educational daisy chain (if one can excuse this image of heavyweights in a daisy chain): Socrates was a teacher to Plato, who in turn was a teacher to Aristotle. Socrates left no written record of his own work, so his philosophical contributions were made primarily through the writings of his students. In Plato's Socratic dialogues, the author famously developed a series of works that used his old teacher as a character holding court with a variety of bright-eyed students on issues of piety, human nature, and some advanced metaphysics.

Socrates was not only a teacher and philosopher; he was also a dedicated and—to those not charmed by him—endlessly annoying political gadfly, who seems to have gotten a great kick out of mocking the unsteady rule of the somewhat haughty Athenian political class. In 399 B.C., at the age of seventy, Socrates was indicted on charges of corrupting the youth of Athens and of spreading heretical religious beliefs; he had claimed to have a personal "daemon," or spirit, that he relied on for a personal sense of right and wrong, rather than reverently worshipping the gods of the city-state. The conviction might have resulted in only a token fine, but Socrates seems to have taken to the courtroom like an open miker at the Chuckle Hut: He was so irreverent and provocative (he suggested a fitting punishment for himself would be a lifetime of free meals) that he actually ended up with a death sentence. After a month in prison that allowed him some final philosophy sessions and some final good-byes, Socrates carried out his own execution, drinking the famous cup of hemlock, a fatal poison.

Plato's fourth and final Socratic dialogue, the *Phaedo*, details the hours before Socrates' death and contains some deep thinking on the nature of the soul, and on what kind of afterlife might await it. Addressing a roomful of friends, one of whom is the titular Phaedo (Plato doesn't write himself into this particular dialogue), Socrates emphasizes a few crucial points of human existence. When one nervous friend puts forth the idea that what might follow death is absolute nothingness, Socrates offers a series of diverse arguments to prove that the human soul is immortal. (He ends up with a total of four such arguments, mainly because his friends don't buy the first three.) Once that immortality is established, there's the question of the afterlife to be dealt with.

Socrates believes any worthy soul passes through the Land of the Dead of Hades to eventually join the company of wise, just, truth-loving gods. He believes he himself will be treated particularly well, and will be allowed to conduct and sit in on what are in essence celestial master classes with all the great minds of history. In fact, Socrates suggests that death is a kind of reward, a chance for the virtuous soul to shed its cumbersome body and move ahead to better things.

But of course not all souls are virtuous. Socrates understands that if death is simply a reward for any life lived, it lets anybody who's lived a wicked life off the hook. So Plato has his old teacher go into a rather in-depth discussion of the process of judgment and damnation that might await a less-than-virtuous soul—that is to say, Socratic hell.

Perhaps the most striking thing about the philosopher's setup is this: Your body is hell. In a theoretical twist that would explain all those late-night infomercials for various ab and bun contraptions, Socrates says that because the plane of the afterlife is so much finer and more wondrous than earthly existence, one of the primary punishments for a wicked soul is to be kicked right back into an earthly, bodily, love-handled existence. Given what a soul is missing out on by not moving forward, a human body is a punishing enough prison for the undeserving.

Before that rebodying, the sorting of the wicked and virtuous takes place in Hades, a vast system of catacombs within the earth that contains a huge lake and four great flowing rivers: one of hot water, one of cold water, one of mud, and one of fire. The rivers all eventually funnel into the drainage dump of Tartarus, pit of pits. Those who are wicked or otherwise unworthy of the rewards of the afterlife, but who still have a chance to get it right, are purified in Hades and sent to live another fleshy life on earth.

But there are those who do not deserve another chance: the incurably wicked. Ah yes, that's what Tartarus is there for. Murderers and committers of great evil are swept up by one of the powerful rivers and spurted right into Tartarus for all eternity.

Socrates, ever the stickler for technicalities, does offer a slight chance for a successful appeal to those damned souls in Tartarus. Once a year, repentant, remorseful souls, who committed their great evil in a moment of great passion, get caught up in the flow of the rivers and are washed out of stinking Tartarus. If, while they are carried along, they see the soul of the person they wronged, they can call out for forgiveness. If forgiveness is granted, they can then crawl out of the rivers and be reprocessed as a not-so-wicked soul. However, if the wronged soul does not grant forgiveness (or maybe pretends not to hear), the river-borne wicked soul gets flushed right back into the pit of pits, to bob there miserably for another year.

Interestingly, Plato also has Socrates expound on the topic of suicide, with Socrates pointing out that it is not possible for a virtuous soul to take its own life in order to shed the body and move to the rewards ahead. That act would instead cancel out the rewards and require a trip back to another body. Socrates is famous as a symbol of dignified suicide, but he makes the distinction that he is not choosing his course of action: he is simply following the commands of the court and, in drinking his cup of hemlock, is acting as an honorable, law-abiding citizen.

MY HELL

MARK MOTHERSBAUGH
Composer, cofounder of Devo, "Spud"

Some people say, "We're in hell already, here on earth," but we should be so lucky to get off that easy. It's got to be infinitely worse—everything evil you've ever done to anybody coming right back at you.

I think punishment would have to be tailored to the sinner. It would have to be a custom job. My personal hell would include unavoidable nausea. That to me is as bad as you can feel physically when your insides are turned upside down and you can't escape them. A horrible feeling. I think my hell would have to involve some way of keeping me in a nauseated state—maybe a terrible roller-coaster ride where you're forced to hold a lidless, plastic container full of used diapers. If you dropped the container, they'd stop the ride and start you over again, faster and with more diapers. Dirtier diapers.

The music you're hearing while you're there is probably that same background stuff you hear in infomercials. Those mindless riffs that are like boll weevils in the brain.

And if the music industry has its own hell, I think it'll be this: Anybody who worked for a record company will be forced to sit with a list of all the decisions they made along the way. And finally, for once, they will be held accountable. There will be no more failing upward.

UNLUCKY SEVEN

One of the most concise and enduring lists of behaviors that can point you toward hell is the seven deadly sins:

pride, greed, sloth, lust, anger, gluttony, and envy. The seven sins contain a bit of overstatement in their name— it's not that each of these sins causes soul-killing damnation in and of themselves, but they are the gateway sins that lead toward spiritual death. Once you've committed one, you are forthrightly headed in the direction of damnation. The Catholic church refers to these sins as Capital Sins, the sins that get a soul kick-started on the road to wickedness.

The seven deadly sins never appear as a formalized list in the Bible, though all are considered separately at some point in scripture. The sins have been ranked in various order by various theologians, and there's a good deal of overlap among them (it's not unusual for a television commercial to pack all seven into thirty seconds). But pride has always stood apart as the deadliest of deadly sins, and while in common parlance pride may not actually sound very sinful, it has a rotten reputation. It was, after all, pridefulness that caused Satan to rebel against God and consequently fall from heaven.

Why seven sins? It's not entirely clear, but the number often turns up as a numeral with otherworldy power (seven viewable planets of the ancient world, seven gates to the Babylonians' Kurnugia, the seven seals of Revelation). The seven deadly slots were not always filled by the same sins; at times, vainglory and apathy were listed, and in the sixth century, when Pope Gregory the Great attempted to codify the list in his *Moralia in Job*, he included sadness rather than sloth. On other's lists, covetousness and avarice turn up as alternate terms for greed. Eventually, vainglory was folded into pride, and sloth was seen to cover sadness and apathy. The list was further reinforced in the thirteenth century when it was discussed in Thomas Aquinas's influential treatise *Summa Theologiae*.

NICE DOGGY

The netherworld needs no alarm system—it's got Cerberus, the watchdog of hell. He was first given his damnable home by the Greeks (and was later adopted by the Romans), serving fiercely and proudly as Hades' best friend. Traditionally, Cerberus is pictured with three heads, although sometimes he is described as having fifty or a hundred heads, along with a back full of snake heads and, for good measure, a dragon's head as a tail. Prowling about the banks of the river Styx, hell's boundary, Cerberus would keep out any nosy mortals trying to get a look at the under-world, and would gobble up any souls trying to get out. The pooch was not infallible though. Heracles wrestled him to a draw, and Orpheus got him to curl up and take a nap by playing some sweet lyre tunes. In Roman tales, Aeneas and Sibyl got past him by drugging him with a poppy-seeded honeycake. Apparently the power of poppies wasn't always necessary: Goddess of beauty Psyche got past Cerberus simply by toss-ing the snack-loving mutt a barleycake.

POINT OF ORIGEN

Origen, a third-century Christian scholar, was a figure of courage who faced down Roman persecution to spread the teachings of the church. However, he got into trouble within the church for propositioning that hell might not be perma-nent. Some of the important questions he raised about the workings of hell deserve further examination here.

Origen was born in Alexandria around A.D. 185 and died somewhere around A.D. 254. His father was killed as a result of Roman emperor Septimius Severus's ongoing oppression of the early Christians. That loss only seems to have steeled Origen's faith. Origen went on to become the guiding force behind his city's Christian school, which, with studies centered on theology and a defense of the Christian faith, was a constant target of malevolence. Somehow, Origen avoided prison (or worse), though he was an active advocate for accused fellow Christians. He seems to have developed the cachet and popularity of an underground rock star, for he had a widespread and fervent following among students.

Origen took Christian doctrine extremely seriously, so seriously that in accordance with some New Testament scripture (". . . there be eunuchs, which have made themselves eunuchs for the kingdom of heaven's sake" (Matt. 19:12)) the young teacher castrated himself. At the time, he wanted to be able to tutor women without any suspicion of lustfulness. Alas, in later writing, he wondered whether he may have acted a bit rashly on this point.

Postcastration, Origen traveled widely, continuing to write and teach. In some areas he was greeted with wild welcome; in others he was considered an upstart and a troublemaker. He was as likely to be reprimanded by church leader as by the Romans.

So what were the doctrinal hot buttons that Origen pushed? Mostly, they concerned hell.

Origen worked hard to fit together the biblical concepts of apocalypse, salvation, and damnation. He believed that hell existed and that it was a place of torment for those who deserved it. But he didn't think it could be eternal. He reasoned that if hell continued to exist after the Apocalypse, the Second Coming of Christ, and the very end of time, then in some ways Satan had scored at least the small triumph of having maintained his bit of turf to rule over. And if hell existed on Satan's terms, that led to questions about God's omnipotence. Origen believed immortal souls could move in two directions, heavenward or hellward, and that eventually all souls, including that of Satan (who after all had once been an angel), would repent and rise to heaven. An infinite God would embrace all these souls as a part of him, leaving no hell to burn.

It turned out this wasn't a very popular idea. Origen's take on hell earned him banishment, a defrocking, and heresy charges in his own time, and he continued to be denounced at church councils and synods for centuries after his death. While today he is considered an important church founder, his "universalist" views are still controversial.

For all the outrage he provoked, Origen seems to have had a nearly miraculous ability to avoid bodily harm (not counting the self-neutering). But that luck did not hold through to the end of his life. During a fresh wave of violent persecutions in 250 at the command of Emperor Decius, Origen was imprisoned and tortured. The Romans did not want to kill Origen—they wanted him to renounce his faith. But despite chain whippings, isolation, torture by fire, and the breaking of his legs in stocks, Origen would not speak against Christianity. He was eventually freed from prison, but he died a few years later due to complications from the injuries he sustained.

His teachings on hell make it unlikely that Origen was vengeful by nature, but he did live long enough to witness a bit of cosmic justice. Conquest-minded Decius, leading a Roman army through some eastern European swamplands, refused to accept the surrender of a nearly vanquished army of Goths, preferring to crush them completely. This refusal fired up the almost-beaten Goths so much that they regrouped and battled back fiercely, defeating the Roman army and slaughtering Decius in the process.

IN THE HOUSE

The workings of hell have been made shockingly, viscerally apparent through the tradition of hellhouses, religious reinterpretations of the classic Halloween haunted house. Typically, a hellhouse presents a series of tableaus, each of which demonstrates, in often graphic and gory detail, the wages of sin. People who attend a hellhouse walk through the various skits and scenarios of hellish transgression, and after witnessing the final horrors that might await an unrepentant soul, are offered a chance at salvation by accepting Jesus as Lord and Savior.

The tradition stretches back at least to 1972, when the Jerry Falwell–founded Liberty University in Lynchburg, VA, began hosting its annual Scaremare. In the early 1990s, Keenan Roberts, an Assemblies of God minister in Colorado, began staging elaborate, intensely produced hellhouses of his own design; by 1995, he was selling Hell House Outreach kits to churches and community groups interested in staging a hell for themselves. The kits come complete with scripts, sound effects, guides to effective prop making, and promotional materials.

Roberts's style of hellhouse makes no attempt to sugarcoat the results of sinfulness, opting instead for shock value: Homosexuality is decried through the enactment of an AIDS funeral; a young woman writhes in agony during an abortion; a drunk driver kills his own family; a satanic ritual ends in human sacrifice. Hellhouse rooms may also present staged enactments of such wickedness as rape, teen suicide, domestic abuse, drug use, and the rave subculture. A climactic hell tableau evokes the sights, sounds, and even smells of the place, and makes it clear that all sinners end up in a realm of never-ending torment. A final heaven scene offers the option of eternal reward for those who repent in time.

Hellhouses have stirred a fair amount of controversy even within Christian churches. Some church leaders worry that Jesus's message is twisted when people are only terrified into accepting it, and others are concerned that those who attend a hellhouse may find the gory spectacle more memorable than the moral instruction; of course, for centuries these same reservations have been part of the debate over how hell should be preached. Despite the controversy, however, hellhouses continue to expand, both in number and in production value.

In 2004, a collective of writers, actors, and comics in Los Angeles bought a Hell House kit and staged Hollywood Hell House, a deadpan, word-for-word parody that featured Bill Maher as Satan and Andy Richter as Jesus. Keenan Roberts may not have been thrilled to have his hellhouse hijacked by Hollywood, but according to a number of press reports, he saw the LA staging as an unusual but welcome opportunity for ministry. In fact, he was in the audience on opening night.

ON THE LIST?

Saul of Tarsus was a Christian-persecuting, itinerant preacher and part-time tent maker whose life was completely transformed in one spectacular biblical moment: While on the road to Damascus, he encountered a blinding vision of Jesus Christ. Christ asked Saul why he was persecuting Christians, and when the startled traveler couldn't come up with much of an answer, he was told to move ahead to Damascus and await further word. Three days later, after his eyesight was returned, Saul began a new life as the Apostle Paul—a primary evangelizer of Jesus's teachings, an enthusiastic missionary, and the early Christian church's first significant theologian.

Paul did not stress the idea of fiery, eternal damnation, but several times in his writings he listed those people who would not gain admittance to the kingdom of God (if one was not admitted to the kingdom, the alternative, at best, was death and annihilation). Paul's list included fornicators, idolaters, adulterers, male prostitutes, sodomites, thieves, the greedy, drunkards, revilers, robbers, impure persons, sorcerers, and those consumed by strife, jealousy, anger, and envy. It's a long enough list to make a lot of sinners nervous, but Paul was very clear about a better option: By accepting the salvation of Jesus Christ, a soul can be redeemed and will live forever. Otherwise, as Paul put it bluntly in Romans 6:23, "The wages of sin is death."

BE BAD, GO TO HEAVEN

Origen's teachings on the Christian idea of hell may have been controversial, but he's managed to hold his place in history as an important and seriously considered church father. Not quite so the case with a contemporary of his, a fellow named Carpocrates, who promoted an emphatically radical notion of the where, what, and why of hell.

Carpocrates was a second-century Alexandrian teacher and philosopher who considered himself a Christian, but who rejected orthodox church teaching in favor of Gnosticism, a belief that there is a form of universal, mystical wisdom available only to a few who pursue it. In the first few centuries A.D., orthodox Christians and Gnostics disagreed vehemently on everything from the way creation had taken place to the nature of Jesus, but Carpocrates' views on hell were a particularly heated departure from mainstream doctrine.

According to Carpocrates, the earth itself was hell, already under the rule of the devil, and human bodies were nothing more than individual prison cells for souls. The soul's struggle to achieve "gnosis"—ultimate oneness/knowledge—and to rise to a noncorporeal, heavenly existence was constantly hampered by the wants and desires of the flesh. Sex, sweets, gold—the hunger for these things is what keeps you in earthly hell.

Therefore—and here Carpocrates came up with one hell of a therefore—the way to defeat the devil and move out of the earthly realm was to sin as prodigiously as possible. That's right—a soul that allowed its human shell to indulge all its overstoked carnal desires would no longer be distracted by those desires, and could move onward and upward. Plainly, if you weren't hungry for sin anymore, you'd stop sinning. And the devil, whose primary function was to tempt a soul into sin, would have no leverage with a soul whose body had already experienced every possible form of excess and depravity. To Carpocrates and his ostensibly hard-partying followers, accepted mainstream codes of morality were simply a trick of the devil. By fooling you into thinking that sinfulness was bad, he was keeping you locked in a cycle of hell on earth.

Today, the Carpocratian's "I'm doing this horrible, pleasurable thing in order to get to heaven" approach sounds like a particularly cunning bit of fun-seeking rationalization. But it's hard to say just how far the Carpocratians put their beliefs into practice (stairway of orgies to heaven?) because most of what we know about Carpocrates and his fellow Gnostics comes to us through the writings of his contemporaneous detractors. Irenaeus, for one—a second-century bishop and a formative theologian of the early church—spent a chapter of his *Against Heresies* decrying Carpocrates, considering him an accomplished sorcerer and fornicator, but not much of a Christian.

THREE-HOUR CRUISE, SEVEN DEADLY SINS

Some fans of the memorably high-concept, dopily absurdist sitcom *Gilligan's Island* have put forth the theory that each of the show's characters represents one of the seven deadly sins. The characters and sins match up as follows:

- **Gilligan:** gluttony (though he remained slight of frame, he was a voracious eater).
- **The skipper:** anger (consider how many times he swatted "little Buddy" Gilligan).

- **Mrs. Howell:** sloth (too used to being catered to by servants).
- **Mr. Howell:** greed (obviously how he became a millionaire).
- **Ginger:** lust (she exhibited it and induced it).
- **Mary Ann:** envy (of Ginger).
- **The professor:** pride (his faith in science never did get the castaways off the damn island).

MANICHAEAN DEBATABLE

What happens to hell when religions collide? One example can be found in the life of Mani, a third-century Persian preacher who drew upon Buddhism, Zoroastrianism, Christianity, and the writings of Plato to found his own religion, Manichaeism.

Manichaeans considered themselves followers of Christ, but did not accept the God of the Old Testament as their God. They also considered Buddha and Zoroaster to be holy. Mani (the word is an honorific—the preacher's personal name is unknown) proposed a dualistic cosmos that was gripped in a fierce battle between material forces of evil and spiritual forces of good. Matter was from the kingdom of darkness and was under the purview of Satan; the heavens were the realm of light, ruled by God. Mani taught that through a life of clean asceticism—with particular care to avoid sexual distraction—a person's soul could accumulate enough light within to move a step up to a higher realm, a temporary paradise ruled by other fully enlightened souls.

For those not headed in an upward direction, the Manichaean notion of hell combined the Gnostic notion of hell on earth and the Buddhist cycle of reincarnation with some Christian apocalyptic hellfire. Souls that had indulged their material nature and weighted themselves down with darkness would, instead of reaching a paradise, be reincarnated for another earthly attempt at living in the light, confined to the imprisoning hell of a human body (Do these pants make me look damned?). There was no limit on how many reincarnations a soul might go through, but there was a time constraint: Those who had not properly repented of their darker sides by the time of Christ's return would be plunged into an earth-consuming fire that would burn until a final moment of cosmic annihilation. At that point, darkness, matter, and the burning, wicked souls would cease to exist, while the souls of light would move on from their temporary paradise to join God in a final, eternal one.

SINFUL CULTURE

The final collaboration between composer Kurt Weill and lyricist Bertolt Brecht, completed in 1933, was *The Seven Deadly Sins*. Brecht and Weill had previously parted ways full of ill will after a dispute over management of the profits earned by their *Threepenny Opera*. But when Weill could not manage to convince Jean Cocteau to work as his librettist, he and Brecht teamed up once more. A young George Balanchine choreographed the show. The *Sins* story follows a central character, Anna, who is split into two personas, one practical, one impulsive. Anna sets out on a journey through America that has her encountering all seven sins; her impulsive side is always willing to indulge, and her practical side reins her back in. The story takes a satirical poke at American attitudes: It turns out that vices can be virtues, and vice versa. And Brecht and Weill's final message is pretty clear: In a capitalist society, the wages of sin is success.

TEMP HELL

In religions that promote the idea of reincarnation rather than eternal damnation, a soul gets some welcome second chances at living a decent, heaven-worthy human life. But sometimes the process of reincarnation has some additional burdens. In certain Hindu sects, it is believed that a mortal must answer not only for his own sins but also for sins passed down through generations by fathers and forefathers ("My Dad lived a life of sin, and all I got was this lousy karma"). Inherited sin is not as much a worry for women, as some believe they cleanse themselves of past sins through the process of menstruation. (In the Hindu text Bhagavata Purana, menstruation is the burden women accept in order to help shed the sin of the sky god Indra, who murdered a holy Brahman. Their payment in return is undiminished sexual desire.)

There are generally two paths a Hindu soul might follow after death. Depending on a soul's degree of sinfulness, the time of death, the thoughts a mortal was focused on at the time of death, and the degree to which proper funeral rites are observed, that soul will either walk a path of light to heavenly reward, or a path of darkness to some disciplinary hell time. Hell-worthy sins can range from the killing of those old sinful parents to pet abuse, and Hindu versions of hell can have scores of subhells, each one set up with fairly specific punishments for a soul's primary sin. A soul may even have to do time in a number of separate hells to clear its record of separate sins. Some hells make a point of fitting the punishment to the crime: Those guilty of rampant lustfulness have their leering eyes pecked out by sharp-beaked birds, and liars might have their tongues sliced away by the tips of frenzied swords.

The Mahabharata, the ancient, epic foundational text of Hinduism, describes a variety of torments that await the sinful and unrighteous, and the penalties are often steep. For instance, for what one would assume to be the relatively minor sin of ingratitude, the offender will go straight to hell, where he will be struck with clubs, hammers, mallets, and heated metal balls. He will be repeatedly impaled with lances. He will then be dragged through forests of sword blades, across hot desert sands, and through some particularly thorny thornbushes. Then to kick the point home, he will be reincarnated as vile vermin.

And there's the rub in the Hindu reincarnation

cycle: Though hell is temporary, one might have to live through some difficult and unpleasant animal lives before getting another chance at humanity. According to the Mahabharata, a priest who commits sacrilege, upon being reincarnated, would have to live as a worm for ten years, a donkey for five years, a hog for five years, a rooster for five years, a jackal for five years, and then a dog for one year before being reincarnated in human form again.

MY HELL

ANDY KINDLER
Comic, actor, "Jew"

I was halfheartedly raised Jewish by parents who were religiously on the fence. At temple the rabbi never mentioned hell. He didn't bring up heaven either, so that was a wash. Jews don't believe in hell. We have experienced enough aggravation right here in this world without worrying about a future place to suffer. Our philosophy is "Don't get your hopes up."

HOTTER IN AUGUSTINE

Augustine, a fourth-century theologian, scholar, writer, and bishop of Hippo (a city in what would be modern-day Algeria), was one of Christianity's earliest, most ardent, and most influential proponents of hell as a very real place of eternal, fiery damnation. As important as he was to the church of his day and as significant as his teachings have been for the Catholic, Protestant, and Eastern Orthodox churches, Augustine spent almost the first half of his life on a path that was anything but heaven-bound.

Augustine was born in 354, and raised in a Roman-controlled area of northern Africa. Augustine's father was a pagan, and though his mother had some affinity for the Christian church, Augustine was not baptized at birth. Augustine was an exceptional young student, and when he reached sixteen, his parents decided to send him off to Carthage in order to further his studies. Augustine made it to that bustling city, but it quickly became clear that his family did not have the funds to secure him the education they desired. So, while money was raised, Augustine did what many a junior abroad has done, availing himself of as much sinfulness and immorality as he could handle (which, according to his self-penned *Confessions*, seems to have been a considerable amount). Augustine lived as a sensualist, indulging the wills and whims of the flesh and fathering an out-of-wedlock son along the way (he did remain quite devoted to the child and its mother). Remarkably, he managed to balance his dissolute lifestyle with some serious scholarly pursuits, and his reputation as a great student, writer, and thinker started to outshine his reputation as a party guy.

Augustine also developed a strong sense of faith, and the religious doctrine he found most appealing was that of Manichaeism. For nine years, he was a devoted Manichaean and a strong promoter of its philosophy and theology. During this time he was also emphatically scornful of Christianity. But during a year in Rome he experienced a powerful change of heart. More and more, Manichaeism began to seem to him to be based on super-stition and mysticism rather than rational thought and coherent philosophy. At the hands of such teachers as Ambrose, bishop of Milan and a father of the early church, Augustine began to drift toward Christian think-ing. Just before Easter of 387, at the age of thirty-three, Augustine was baptized a Christian. When his mother, who had served as his confidante and traveling compan-ion, died shortly afterward, Augustine threw himself into his new religion with a convert's passion that reshaped the entire church.

As a Christian, Augustine celebrated the beauty of the natural world—God's creation—but he stressed the price that humankind had paid by committing original sin. And for Augustine original sin was explicitly sexual in nature; it was not simply the idea that Adam and Eve had defied God in the Garden of Eden. Original sin specifically stemmed from the lust and pleasure with which Adam and Eve had approached sexual intercourse after they had eaten the fruit of the tree of knowledge. Augustine saw sexual immorality as the primary indicator of humanity's fallen nature, and he believed that such wickedness was inherent and unavoidable. At times, he argued that even monogamous married couples were at risk of immoral behavior if they felt any pleasure while procreating.

Despite Augustine's own free-wheeling background (and with a bit of the zealousness of a new vegetarian raging against the perils of beef), the theologian warned vehemently about the consequences of human sinfulness. In his massively influential treatise *City of God*, Augustine argued that any soul not baptized into Christianity and accepting of the undeserved salvation offered by Jesus Christ would go to hell. And Augustine's hell was a real place of fire and brimstone, in which both the physical bodies of humans and the spirit bodies of demons would be tormented.

Augustine also developed a detailed and comprehensive system of hell's setup that sought to answer some lingering Christian debates about the place. Some had argued that hell could not be a realm of eternal damnation because the bodies there would be consumed by the fire long before eternity played out. Augustine answered that hellfire was capable of causing suffering without causing obliteration. Some had argued that eternity was too long a punishment for sins that had happened in a moment of moral misstep. Augustine answered that sin could not be judged by its duration, but by its consequence. Original sin may have been the result of one passionate moment, but it had caused the fall of humanity and deserved a punishment of eternal damnation.

There had long been some question as to how hell would differ before and after the Second Coming of Christ, and Augustine took this on by developing a concept that would eventually become a crucial part of hell's architecture: purgatory. Augustine did not use that specific term, but he believed there were several ways a soul might be handled after death. Those who had come to salvation would rise to heaven. Those who were unbaptized or who were unrepentantly wicked would sink to hell. A middle group contained those who were not quite completely good, and those who were not quite completely evil. The not-quite-good might eventually rise to heaven after the Last Judgment, having served purgatorial time in a slightly less miserable area of hell (the phrase for this was *tolerabilior fiat ipsa damnatio*, "a more tolerable damnation"). The not-quite-evil would also do time in this state of slightly more tolerable damnation, but if unrepentant or still otherwise unworthy at the time of the Last Judgment, they would sink into the full flames of hell. The milder hells and the chance of redemption only existed prior to the Last Judgment. After that, there were only two, eternal realms—heaven and hell—and there were only two groups of souls: the saved and the damned.

HOW LOW MUST YOU GO?

In the wake of Augustine's teachings, a couple of nagging questions developed for the church: If baptism and acceptance of Jesus Christ as the Savior were necessary for salvation, what happened to infants who died before they had a chance to be baptized? And what happened to all the virtuous souls who lived and died before the time of Jesus? The answer took the form of another spiritual realm: limbo. Limbo was no paradise, but it was no hell either. Though never a part of official church doctrine, early theologians and believers began to shape a cosmology in which there was a place just below heaven that could hold the souls of those who were virtuous but had not fulfilled the requirements for salvation. They would be suspended in a neutral state until the final judgment, after which they would be accepted into heaven.

In time, limbo (from the Latin *limbus*, "border") separated into two limbos. There was the Limbo of Children, specifically for those unbaptized infants, and the Limbo of the Fathers, for those worthy souls who had lived and died before Christ's Resurrection.

Leaders of the Protestant Reformation saw no scriptural support for the existence of any limbo, and thoroughly rejected it.

In contemporary times, belief in limbo has been greatly downplayed, leaving the realm in something of a limbo of its own.

LOWERING THE BAR

The limbo, a dance in which dancers bend their bodies backward to pass under an incrementally lowered stick, is derived from a funeral dance performed on the Caribbean islands of Trinidad and Tobago. The dance was originally intended to assist and encourage a departed loved one's soul to move on from the state of limbo to a happier afterlife.

The limbo was a hot pop-chart phenomenon in 1962. Chubby Checker, who'd had a number one hit in 1961 with "The Twist," reached number two with "Limbo Rock." The Capris, a Queens, New York, vocal group, cracked the top hundred with "Limbo." And instrumental aces the Champs ("Tequila") charted with both a Chubby-less "Limbo Rock" and the straightforwardly named "Limbo Dance."

MY HELL

JEANINE BASINGER

Author, film historian, Chair of Film Studies Department at Wesleyan University

Everyone in academia knows what form their hell might take: It would be an eternal faculty meeting. One hundred or more people who have different agendas sit in a room and can't agree on what to do—so they discuss it. And discuss it. And discuss it. And discuss it. And then they decide to table it and discuss it at a later date. Altogether, the one hundred or more people, while doing all this discussing, generate enough energy to power a very small kitchen appliance. Like a toaster. This is hell, believe me.

As for specific punishments, film scholars who have used the words "diegetic," "hierarchy of informational communication," and "projected penis misrepresentational replacement" when writing about movie musicals have to watch army training films for all eternity.

PURGING

The idea of purgatory—a third place, not heaven or hell, in which a repentant soul might endure temporary punishment and have a chance to atone for its sins—slowly took shape throughout medieval times. This third option gained status both through ongoing theological debate and through a great degree of wishful/hopeful thinking on the part of believers. As the idea of a final judgment based on individual actions took hold, those who knew they were not sin-free and thus probably not heaven-bound, desperately wanted to believe in some other option than outright damnation. Purgatory was recognized by the church (after significant debate) at the First and Second Councils of Lyons (conducted in 1245 and 1274, respectively). A belief in purgatory was formalized in 1439 by the decree of union at the Council of Florence.

Long-simmering divisions in the Christian church came to a head with the Protestant Reformation in the early 1500s. Protestants—Martin Luther chief among them—came to reject a good deal of entrenched church doctrine, including the existence of purgatory. In response, the leaders of the Catholic church collected themselves for the nearly twenty-year-long Council of

Trent (begun in 1545), during which Catholic doctrine, including the existence of purgatory, was emphatically reaffirmed. After Trent, purgatory's purpose, method, topography, and even its temperature were made clear.

Yes, there was hellfire in purgatory, the purpose of which was not to torment but to burn the sins from a soul in a process of purification. The heat and strength of the fire was exactly equivalent to the degree of one's sinfulness. A soul, though immaterial, would experience the flames as physical pain. But in the end all those condemned to purgatory would eventually achieve salvation.

ZONED

Among the 156 episodes of the classic 1960s TV show *The Twilight Zone*, creator Rod Serling presented several stories that centered on deals with the devil, and dozens that presented hellish situations. But one episode in particular revealed how hell itself might work. In "A Nice Place to Visit," actor Larry Blyden played Rocky Valentine, a rude, crude burglar who is shot and killed mid-heist by a police officer. Rocky regains consciousness to find that not only is he uninjured, but he is now set to live a stylish afterworld high life. He's in a swinging, swanky pad and is attended to by a remarkably solicitous valet named Pip (Sebastian Cabot). Rocky is shocked to find himself in paradise, but quickly adapts to his surroundings. The women he meets are beautiful and eager to please, the cops are easily frightened midgets, and fine food and drink are always available. Every roll of the dice comes up in his favor, every hand of cards is a winner, and every time he plays a slot machine, he hits a jackpot. But as good luck and fine living become grindingly predictable, Rocky becomes bored and irritable. He summons Pip and lets him know that while he appreciates the time in heaven, he thinks he'd be more comfortable in hell. Can Pip arrange a transfer? Pip just laughs. Rocky's already there.

INDULGENT

If individuals were virtuous enough to recognize they had committed a sin, and sorry enough to repent of it, was there anything they could do while still alive to lessen the sting of the purgatory that awaited? The answer came in the form of indulgences, which began as simple expressions of hope and faith, but which became the center of a wildly corrupt cash business, and a major catalyst of the Reformation.

Technically, an indulgence is the remission of temporal punishment for a sin that has been forgiven: that is, a kind of church-granted time off for good behavior (actually time off for good reflection upon bad behavior). Originally, the indulgence was intended as a time-saver in terms of penance only—a church was allowing a sinner to make amends for his or her sin (through prayer or good works) in less time than might have normally been the case. But for many worshippers and in many churches, the indulgence came to represent not time saved for the living, but actual hours, days, or months sliced off the time that a soul would otherwise spend in purgatory.

These were "partial" indulgences, available to believers who would follow the church's instructions on the matter. By the end of the eleventh century, the widespread acceptance of the partial indulgences had led to the availability of complete, or "plenary," indulgences, which meant that no time at all would be spent in purgatory. These were first developed as a kind of military recruiting incentive as the first expeditions of the

Crusades were waged: Pope Urban II declared that crusaders who had confessed their sins and then died in battle would skip purgatory and go straight to heaven.

In 1300, Pope Boniface VIII declared that year to be the first of the church's "Jubilee" years, and announced that any believer making a pilgrimage to Rome and following some church guidelines on the confession of sins would receive full pardon of those sins. This Jubilee year offer of indulgence was emphatically received, and Rome was regularly packed with thousands of pilgrims. But as the idea of indulgences spread, the practice was often abused, sometimes taking the form of a cash-for-penance business. By the middle of the fifteenth century, some believers might have felt that purgatory existed only for those who couldn't afford to buy their way out of it (though the well-to-do faithful may have thought they were still getting a bargain). Pope Sixtus IV served from 1471 to 1484, and while he gets all due credit for sponsoring the construction of the Sistine Chapel, he also extended the reach of indulgences by declaring that they could now be purchased by friends and family on behalf of those already in purgatory. In other words, you could buy your favorite deceased relatives out of the place.

Things reached a critical point in 1517, when

Pope Leo X made indulgences available to those who contributed to a reconstruction fund for St. Peter's Basilica in Rome. Johann Tetzel, a Dominican priest who had become the commissioner for all indulgences in Germany, marketed these indulgences so brazenly that it is believed his hard-sell approach led directly to Martin Luther's famous opening shot of the Reformation, the list of complaints against church doctrine and practices, known as the Ninety-five Theses.

Many within the church had been equally disgusted by the widespread sale of indulgences, and when Catholicism reaffirmed its official beliefs at the Council of Trent, it was made clear that while indulgences could still be part of church practice, they were to be treated as a strictly controlled form of spiritual assistance rather than as a for-profit business.

NETHER THERMODYNAMICS

How hot is hell? While the scriptures don't provide a specific temperature, science provides a maximum possible temperature of 832 degrees Fahrenheit. That figure comes from the descriptions of hell as a lake of fire and brimstone.

Brimstone—sulfur—can only be maintained in a liquid state up to 832 degrees Fahrenheit. Above that temperature, it vaporizes. Of course, that calculation only applies in situations of normal atmospheric pressure. If hell has a more highly pressurized atmosphere—from packing all those souls into a confined space—its temperature could be considerably higher.

INFERNAL

Perhaps nowhere has the scene in hell been described with more detail or more artistry than in Dante's *Inferno*, the first section of his three-part *Divine Comedy* (the other sections are *Purgatorio* and *Paradiso*). Dante's *Inferno*, written over most of the decade between 1310 and 1320, brought hell to life with a remarkably detailed geology and architecture. It provided readers with all the details they might want on hell's sights, sounds, smells, and torments, as well as the identities of many of the tormentors and tormented. An understanding of Dante's life is crucial to understanding the inferno he constructed; here was a guy who ended up with some serious scores to settle, and he settled them brilliantly in his netherworldly writing.

Dante Alighieri was born in Florence in 1265, the son of a prominent family that had loyalties to one faction of the rather cutthroat local political scene. As a kid, Dante may have grown used to the sight of wild, bloody brawls in the streets. It is believed that as a young man Dante pursued his education through the public schools of Florence, picking up a mastery of Latin and a deep appreciation of ancient classical poets such as Ovid, Homer, and especially Virgil.

When Dante was nine years old, he met and fell deeply and passionately in love with the woman who would become his lifelong muse. Never mind that the muse was only eight at the time. She was Beatrice, the quiet, pretty daughter of a wealthy Florentine banker. Because of the difference in status between Beatrice's affluent family and Dante's somewhat less affluent family, he had no hope of courting his would-be love, and by the time both of them were young adults, they were each wed to more socially acceptable spouses. In fact, Dante may have only spoken to Beatrice a few times in his life, most significantly at the party where he first met her and, years later, when she sent his heart racing by greeting him on the street. But as Dante began to write poetry, Beatrice was the feminine ideal that quickened his pulse, and he used his art to give voice to his unwavering love and his sense of awe at her beauty. When she died in 1290, Dante was devastated, and he attempted to fight off his sorrows by diving deeper into his studies and his writing. But these distractions didn't help much. His devotion to his muse continued until the end of his life, and sweet Beatrice turns up as both a helpful figure in the *Inferno*, and as a memorably "radiant and comforting" guide through heaven in *Paradiso*.

By 1295, Dante was a blossoming poet, but he had also begun a career in politics, serving in several capacities on the varied city councils of Florence. Unfortunately, these positions put him in the middle of the city's escalating *Sopranos*-like turf wars, and in 1302, after he had spoken against Pope Boniface VIII for the papacy's taking sides in city disputes, he found himself convicted of charges akin to fiscal mismanagement and insubordination. The charges were probably trumped up, but the punishment was real. Dante was banished from Florence, a city he had loved but would never return to.

Dante spent the rest of his life living in Tuscany, Verona, and Ravenna, often counting on the support and kindnesses of noblemen familiar with his work. He worked on the *Divine Comedy* through these years, but also had time to write a number of diatribes aimed at the leaders of Florence. The city offered him amnesty in 1315, with a few strings attached. Dante could come back home if he would pay a fine, march through the city in a ritual of public humiliation, and serve a term of incarceration. Dante declined the offer.

He completed the *Divine Comedy* in early 1321, but did not live long enough to see what a massively popular and influential work it would become. On a trip between Venice and Ravenna, he contracted malaria and died in September of that year.

HOT, HOT, HOT

According to the *Tabasco PepperFest Cookbook*, Dante's Inferno Salsa gets its heat from 2½ tablespoons of Tabasco Habanero Pepper Sauce.

CIRCULAR REASONING

The *Inferno* is a first-person account of a travel through hell, with the author guided through the underworld by an old poetic favorite, Virgil. Geographically, Dante's hell might be imagined in the shape of a huge, conical sinkhole opening deep into the earth, with the cone coming to its point at the lowest pit of hell. From gateway to pit there are nine descending levels—the nine circles of hell—each growing more hellish as the journey spirals downward. Dante describes each level with the heart of a poet and the eye of a city planner, detailing everything from hell's moat-and-trench sewage systems to its finely honed torments (and there is some overlap between those two).

At the beginning of the poem, the author is in the throes of a deep, depressive, middle-age crisis, besieged by forces of spiritual uncertainty (which appear in the frightening, allegorical form of wild beasts). He is on the wrong path, both literally and figuratively lost. At the behest of an angelic Beatrice, the ghost of Virgil joins the author to take him on a pilgrimage to find God (and Beatrice), a trip that will take them through hell, purgatory, and heaven.

Virgil and the author step through the gates of hell, which bear the homey inscription, "Abandon all hope, ye who enter here." The first souls the pair encounter are in a kind of infernal foyer. These are people with serious commitment issues—they could not commit to a life of enough good or evil to qualify them for heaven or hell. Now they spend their time chasing an unmarked (uncommitted) flag while they are stung by wasps and bitten by worms. Dante feels sorry for them, but he is powerfully disgusted all the same.

Hell's ferryman, Charon, floats the pair across the river Acheron, the official boundary to hell's real estate. On the other side, they begin their journey through hell proper, eventually visiting all nine circles.

First circle: This is limbo, home to worthy, virtuous pagan souls. In fact, it's the circle that Virgil is currently calling home. Dante doesn't get into the question of unbaptized infants, but he does allow himself some time here for chitchat with some of the great poets who lived and died before the time of Christ: Ovid, Horace, and Lucan.

Second circle: Here, those who could not control their lusts and passions are punished by being whirled around in unceasing windstorms. The second circle is also headquarters for the monster Minos, who serves as hell's maître d'. After listening to a sinner's confessions, he wraps his massive tail into coils. The number of coils indicate the circle a sinner is assigned to.

Third circle: Here, those who have lived lives of gluttony must lie in muddy filth and be forever pelted by a rain of garbage and excrement. Their misfortune is overseen by a canine enforcer, Cerberus, the three-headed hell-hound. The growling, limb-gnawing beast makes sure that every soul gets properly besplattered.

Fourth circle: Those who hung on to material wealth in a greedy, miserly fashion are forced to face off against those who carelessly frittered away their wealth. The two unhappy teams must roll giant boulders at each other. There is a high proportion of priests on this level.

Fifth circle: This is where the river Styx, the boundary between upper and lower hell, runs. In the river's waters, those who lived lives of gasket-blowing anger assault each other in a hellish mix of aquanastics and demolition derby. Those who lived lives of sloth are stuck in the swampy lands around the river, where they can do little more than spit up mud. Dante begins to spot some familiar faces—political enemies of his are being ripped to pieces.

Sixth circle: The area of lower hell is within the demonic city of Dis, the capital of hell. Once within the city, the travelers discover that the sixth circle is reserved for heretics, who must lie for eternity in flaming graves (again, Dante spots a political rival getting his proper fiery comeuppance).

Seventh circle: After making their way down a steep canyon guarded by a minotaur, the travelers arrive at the seventh circle, reserved for those who have committed crimes of violence. The circle is separated into three rings: In the first ring, those who committed violence against others bob in a river of boiling blood. In the second ring, those who committed suicide have their souls trapped within trees. The third ring is for those who were violent toward God, art, or nature, through respective acts of blasphemy, usury, or homosexuality. All must spend eternity walking circles through a burning wasteland scorched by fiery rains. Dante is saddened to spot one of his early artistic mentors here, walking among the homosexuals (he seems sad about the punishment, not particularly the sexual preference).

Eighth circle: With the aid of the massive, dragonlike monster Geryon, Dante and Virgil make it across a deep abyss to the eighth circle, known as Malebolge, which might be translated as "evil pouches" or "ditches." Various forms of deceit and ill will are punished here, with sinners assigned to one of ten ditches.

- **Pouch one:** Pimps and seducers are whipped by demons.
- **Pouch two:** Flatterers must lie in a stream of crap.
- **Pouch three:** Corrupt church leaders are hung upside down over a corrupted form of a baptismal font while their feet are set afire.
- **Pouch four:** Occultists and fortune-tellers mull about in an understandably aimless fashion—their heads are attached backward.
- **Pouch five:** Reserved for those who accepted bribes—they are boiled in tar and prodded by demons.
- **Pouch six:** Full of hypocrites who must forever walk in circles, in the process trampling upon Caiphas, the priest who pronounced Christ's death sentence.
- **Pouch seven:** Here, there is a particularly gruesome entanglement of thieves and serpents. A thief turns into a serpent when bitten by one, and then must bite another thief to regain human form.
- **Pouch eight:** Deceivers burn in flames. Dante places Greek *Odyssey* hero Ulysses here for coming up with the deception of the Trojan-tricking Trojan horse—Dante and Virgil both having had rooting interest in the Trojan side of things.
- **Pouch nine:** Those who instigated discord and

scandal see their terrible open wounds heal up just in time to be reopened by sword-wielding demons.
- **Pouch ten:** Liars and falsifiers suffer from some awful, unsightly plagues and diseases.

Ninth circle: The lowest region of hell is for traitors, who are separated into four categories:

- Those who betrayed their family stand in a frozen lake, only their heads above the ice.
- Those who betrayed country are frozen up to the tops of their heads.
- Those who betrayed guests (offered false hospitality with hidden agendas) are frozen in the lake on their backs.
- And at the very bottom of hell, in the pit of pits, are those who betrayed great benefactors. Here Dante finds what he considers to be history's greatest traitors. First, frozen waist-deep in the pit, is a huge, beastly three-headed Lucifer, who, having betrayed God, is the traitor of all traitors. Lucifer's heads are chomping away at the greatest human traitors—Judas Iscariot, betrayer of Christ, and Brutus and Cassius, betrayers of Julius Caesar. (These latter two reflect the fact that Dante had

become a proponent of Italian national unity as a curative for corrupt city-states like Florence.)

Here the adventure of the *Inferno* ends, as Dante and Virgil climb over hairy, chomping Lucifer to reach the Lethe, the river of forgetfulness, and scramble out of hell just in time to see sunrise on Easter morning.

ENDNOTE: NOT COMING HOME

Clearly, a fear of hell has not stopped a great number of mortals from becoming intimately acquainted with the details of the place, and a lack of firsthand experience hasn't stopped many from theorizing on the most intricate aspects of hell's inner workings. Elaborate visions of just how damnation works have come from within churches and without, with either sort capable of having a significant, netherworldy impact. For instance, Augustine's writings on hell are still a crucial foundation of Christian beliefs, while Dante's hell survives as both literary classic and deeply embedded cultural touchstone.

And now that we've gotten a sense of definition,

location, and damnation, we can move on to examine some of hell's notable inhabitants—namely, its attendant devils and demons.

But one final word on Mr. Alighieri. In the decades after Dante's death, the *Divine Comedy* came to inhabit a kind of middle ground between the secular and the sacred, celebrated not only as an artistic triumph, but almost as a kind of addendum to scripture. It was a public favorite, and yet it also received the kind of scholarly respect and attention a holy work might command.

Florence, belatedly realizing the error of dissing an important native son, fought to bring Dante's remains back to his hometown.

To no avail.

Today, Florence has the Casa di Dante and the Via Dante Alighieri.

But Dante himself is still in Ravenna.

WHO'S IN CHARGE?

*An apology for the devil: It must be remembered that we have heard
only one side of the case. God has written all the books.*
—Samuel Butler

The devil's cleverest wile is to convince us that he does not exist.
—Charles Baudelaire

Hell, as we've seen, can be an exceedingly complicated place. To keep it running smoothly, what's required is some truly extraordinary leadership at the top (or bottom, if we wish to be more geographically precise).

So, who runs hell?

Well, an exact answer depends on which hell one happens to be asking about, but in general it's safe to say that the evil entity serving as the chief executive officer down below is the one commonly known to us as the devil.

What's the devil like?

Extremely evil. Usually. But mortals of every culture and religion have long speculated on the precise physical and spiritual attributes of the embodiment of ultimate evil. Consequently, devils throughout the ages have taken a soul-boggling variety of shapes, powers, and personas. Hell's ruler has been envisioned as a crafty serpent, a gang leader of genies, a fallen angel, a lord of death, and variously as a god of lies, flies, pain, chaos, and/or excrement. We've also seen that some netherworlds have not been entirely testosterone-driven, and have sometimes been ruled by she-demons, she-beasts, and some very powerful and temperamental goddesses.

In many early religions and early conceptions of hell, the idea of a universal duality—of the battle between good and evil—was not stressed as greatly as it would be later by sixth-century B.C. Persian philosophers (Zoroaster chief among them) and in the beliefs of Jews, Christians, and Muslims.

Before that duality kicked in, many religions developed extensive pantheons of gods that were as unpredictable as humans: That is, they were fickle or moody creatures with a ticklish blend of dark sides and enlightened sides, always capable of either good or evil. In most of these cases the gods who ruled the underworld or the

Land of the Dead were not portrayed as the field generals of all evil in the world, but as fearsome figures possessing dangerous but limited powers—figures who, in overseeing hell, were carrying out a necessary but understandably nasty job.

It was during the first centuries of Christianity that Satan himself was recognized as a singular malevolent force, a supernatural entity who is the fount of all evil. Satan plays a variety of roles in the Hebrew Bible, the Apocrypha, and the New Testament, but the recognizable Satan we've come to know in popular culture developed outside sacred texts, primarily through some mix-and-match borrowing of imagery: hooves from Pan, the Greek god of sexual desire; horns from the Caananites' Moloch; and trident (aka pitchfork) from the Greek and Roman gods of the seas (Poseidon and Neptune, respectively).

At the heart of all conceptions of a devil, there is a recognition of evil, but also a strong theme of otherness. While God generally represents love, goodness, protection, and the power of community, in every culture and religion there is always the figure who represents the dark side, the unexplored realms, the prideful beast who defies the norm—the ultimate adversary of goodness.

Who's in charge of hell?

Let's take a look and, as Cervantes suggested, give some devils their due.

BABYLON'S BEAST

The Babylonians believed that humanity's mixed nature and unreliable behavior were a result of the very stuff the universe is made of—namely, rotting she-dragon flesh.

By 1000 B.C., the Babylonians had developed a creation myth, the *Enuma Elish*, handed down to them from the Sumerians, Phoenicians, and Carthaginians. It went something like this: Tiamat, a powerful she-dragon, existed before time began and was considered to be the ruler of the universe. But when other gods angered her by showing off their powers, her simmering rage turned her from a benevolent creature into a hideous monster. The other gods realized something had to be done about their now fierce and unpredictable ruler, so a fellow named Marduk, the sun-bull, challenged Tiamat to a battle. He promptly defeated her by shoving a great thunderstorm into her mouth to distract and disarm her, and then lancing her belly. When Tiamat died, Marduk expertly carved her up and created the heavens and the earth from her carcass.

That carving is described in the poetry of the creation saga: Two of Tiamat's oversized ribs become the east and the west; her punctured eyes let loose the flow of the Tigris and the Euphrates; her saliva becomes clouds and rain; her tail is curled up into the sky to form all the stars; and her crotch is used to support the heavens (partly cloudy with a chance of groin).

Not a pretty picture. But Marduk isn't quite done. He gets ahold of Tiamat's husband, a lesser god named Kingu, and slices him open as well. From Kingu's blood, Marduk creates humankind.

GODS GONE WILD

Once poor, scaly Tiamat had been sliced and diced to create all of the Babylonian cosmos, another female stepped up to run the Babylonian underworld. We've already met her: Ereshkigal, the princess of the kingdom of shadows. For a time, she reigned freely and solely over the Babylonian hell of Kurnugia, but she was increasingly desirous of a coruler. According to the legends that have survived, Ereshkigal invites Nergal, the god of destruction, to join her in hell (a familiar first date for some of us?). She's got a great night planned, and offers Nergal plenty of food and beer (an ancient Babylonian specialty), but he's not interested. She cuts to the chase and offers up her hellishly fine body to him, and suddenly, yeah, he's interested. They tumble into bed for several days of carnal gymnastics, and Ereshkigal ends up pleased enough to offer Nergal the position of lord of the underworld. He says sure—but, um, he just wants to leave for a while to tell everyone up aboveground what a great gal she is and what a great couple they are. Perhaps against better instincts, Ereshkigal lets him go. And acting as the first morning-after cad in the history of literature, he does not return.

A bitter, frustrated Ereshkigal has to use a demon to fetch her bedmate and bring him back. But when Nergal finally is set up as underworld lord, he is so ineffective in the role that an even more bitter and frustrated Ereshkigal has to take over the realm again. Nergal is consigned to the more ceremonial role of hell's first husband.

In another underworld tale, a bored and still unsatisfied Ereshkigal sets after her brother-in-law, Tammuz, the hunkily handsome god of the harvest. In doing so, Ereshkigal disregards that he is already married to the beautiful Ishtar, whose status as goddess of love and promiscuity (that is, sacred prostitutes) gave her a distinctly formidable set of bedroom skills. Ereshkigal kidnaps Tammuz, but Ishtar follows the pair down to hell. Ishtar must shed an article of clothing at each of the seven gates that lead through the underworld, and she arrives at Ereshkigal's inner sanctum completely naked. There is a confrontation, but Ishtar's sex power can't quite match Ereshkigal's hell power, and Ishtar is slaughtered by Ereshkigal.

A god named Ea then stepped in to work out a compromise: Ishtar would be brought back to life and set aboveground. Tammuz would spend fall and winter warming up Kurnugia with Ereshkigal, and spend spring and summer up on earth canoodling with Ishtar.

Thus, from a devilish underworld tale of lust and jealousy, the Babylonians conjured a fairly nifty explanation of the seasons.

THE DEVIL'S LUNCHBOX

- **Deviled eggs:** Have their origin in ancient Roman recipes for garnished boiled eggs. Thought to have been so named by eighteenth-century foodies.

- **Deviled ham:** The oddly spreadable lunch meat was created in 1868 by the sons of canned-goods pioneer William Underwood. According to the folks at Underwood, the sprightly little devil is the oldest existing trademark still in use in the United States.
- **Devil's food cake:** Sinfully chocolaty these days, devil's food cake has also been the name for a red-dyed cake with white frosting. The first American recipe (for the chocolaty kind) seems to have appeared in the 1902 *Mrs. Rorer's New Cook Book* by the Julia Child of her day, Sara Tyson Rorer.

HOT GREECE

The ancient Greeks borrowed quite a bit of mythology from the civilizations of Mesopotamia and then developed their own twists to the gods and their stories. The Greeks' hell, Hades, was ruled by the eponymous Hades, the ill-tempered brother of the powerful gods Zeus and Poseidon. When the three brothers overthrew their father, the top god Kronos, and drew lots to divvy up the realms they would oversee, Zeus got the sky, Poseidon got the seas, and Hades drew the underworld, which thereafter was known by his name. Hades was considered a god rather than a devil, and he was not the embodiment of death; that title belonged to the shadowy character Thanatos. But while not outright evil, Hades was a strict stickler for underworld justice, and he was a specialist in using his powers to create merciless torments and tortures for anyone he ruled over. He could rip a mortal to shreds when in that sort of mood, but he often delighted in crueler, soul-crushing inflictions. He's the one who came up with the darkly ingenious punishment for Sisyphus, who was forced to continually roll a stone up a hill, only to have his strength give out at the top so that the stone rolled back down, requiring him to begin his futile task once more—and forever. Hades also came up with a dastardly winner for Tantalus, who was put in a permanent state of thirst and hunger, and set neck deep in water with an array of fruits dangling just above his head. Every time he reached for the food or dipped down for the water, they moved just out of reach.

Hades bears some resemblance to later devils of the Faust legends in that he was viewed as a sly and nasty character who served a comeuppance to mortals who mostly deserved it: Sisyphus was a thief, murderer, and mocker of the gods, while Tantalus was such a gourmand that, for a gods' dinner party, he cooked and served his own son to create the fanciest of entrées (Atkins-friendly but unforgivable nonetheless). Hades abducted a female companion for himself, Persephone, who came to be seen as a formidable queen of the underworld. (A deal that allowed Persephone to spend part of the year above-ground provided the basis for a Greek explanation of seasons similar to the Babylonian Ereshkigal stories.)

Hades was feared enough that Greeks wanted a way to refer to him without invoking the name of their hell, so they began to call him Pluto, a reference to the valuable gems and minerals that were part of Hades's underworld kingdom (*ploutus* is Greek for "wealth"). When the Romans appropriated the Greek pantheon of gods, their Hades was ruled by Pluto.

DON'T GO THERE

Humans may battle the devil for their souls, but they've been more than willing to surrender to him quite a few chunks of less-than-choice real estate. Some of the most daunting, inhospitable, and/or out-of-the-way bits of earthly terrain have been granted devilish monikers, including:

- Devil's Slide, California
- Devil's Gate, Wyoming
- Devils Tower, Wyoming
- Devil's Backbone, Maryland
- Devil's Lake, Wisconsin
- Devil's Ditch, England
- Devil's Marbles, Australia

SAY MY NAME

The Aztec hell of Mictlan was run in the manner of a cosmic bed-and-breakfast by the rather kindly albeit somewhat larcenous couple of Mictlantecuhtli and his wife Mictecacihuatl. Aztecs were customarily cremated with their jewelry, fine clothing, perfumes, and assorted valuables, because the greater the bribe they could offer to Mictlantecuhtli and the missus, the swankier the accommodations they would be allowed to enjoy in the afterlife ("Sir, might I offer you this turquoise in exchange for a room with a minibar?"). All Aztec souls, save for those of men who died in battle and those of women who died in childbirth, made the perilous, demon-plagued, four-year journey to Mictlan, but once they arrived there, it was essentially a place of rest.

Things could get a bit ugly in Mictlan too, however. If a particularly sinful soul came before Mictlantecuhtli, he might call upon Xipetotec, the "flayed god," who did double duty as the Aztec overseer of both vegetation and torment. Xipetotec was strongly allied with the underworld, and was always at the ready to flay a misguided soul into penitential submission. When not doing hell work, Xipetotec's regular, earthly day job was split between allowing crops to flourish and inflicting disease, plague, and madness on the living. His nickname is derived from the fact that he was such a devoted fan of excruciating torment that he was given to flaying himself as well (and in a strange twist of dark generosity, it was his own flayed flesh that sometimes helped produce those bountiful crops). Aztec human sacrifices were often offered up to appease the whims of Xipetotec.

DEVILS AU NATUREL

- Devil's claw is an extremely spiky plant and the bane of adventurous hikers. In extract form, it is used to treat gout, arthritis, and menopausal symptoms.
- Devilwood is a small scrub tree related to the olive. It keeps to itself.

MORE HEL

We've seen that the Vikings had a particularly powerful she-devil ruling their icy realm of Niflheim, the goddess whose name was appropriated for the Christian underworld: Hel. A little more on the lady:

This cantankerous goddess was, at best, quaintly unattractive and, at worst, monstrously repugnant. According to Viking legend, Hel was the most ill tempered of all gods, whose dour, scowling countenance even frightened other gods of equal power. Okay, no smile, no personality, howsabout her figure, you ask? Well, Hel's body was relatively normal from the waist up, but below the waist her flesh was decayed and rotting. (Although that top/bottom split description may be the result of some Viking fear-of-strong-female sex panic— there are other descriptions of Hel in which the split is longitudinal—one side of her body from top to bottom is pale white, while the other side is blackened with decay.)

Wherever the rot was, Hel did manage to fit in nicely with her family, mainly because the members of her family were equally horrible. Her father was Loki, the Viking god of deceit and wickedness, and her mother was the monstrous, mortal-hating giant Angrboda. Her older brother, Fenrir, was a huge hungry wolf who was rumored to be capable of swallowing up the world in one sloppy gulp. Her little brother was Jormungand, a giant serpent given to spitting vast amounts of putrid venom all over the earth.

The family was so unpleasant that the other gods, working like an angered condo board, secretly plotted to find a way to kick them out of Asgard, the Viking heaven. Odin, the greatest of the gods, came up with a method of disposal for each of the siblings: Fenrir was bound in strange, unbreakable chains; Jormungand was plunged to the bottom of the ocean with his tail stuck in his mouth; and Hel was kicked out of Asgard directly into the dark and cold of Niflheim.

With Hel's arrival, Niflheim became home to Helheim, a full-fledged hell in which Odin charged the emphatically unsightly goddess with overseeing the souls not only of unslaughtered warriors, but also of evildoers, criminals, and those who had died of unpleasant illnesses. Hel took to her new career with gusto and managed to make the unfriendly climes of Niflheim even more unbearable, not by coming up with new tortures and torments, but by enforcing a strict policy of mind-numbing nothingness. Souls that came to her were made painfully hungry and were condemned to sit in icy darkness with absolutely nothing to do—a situation that must have made eternity feel like even more of an eternity.

The only thing to look at in Helheim was Hel herself, and looking in that direction was always a gut-wrenching mistake.

BAD BROTHER

A pair of old siblings that prefigure Satan can be found in the ancient Egyptian underworld of Duat: the god of the dead, Osiris, and his annoying brother, Seth. Osiris wasn't always a figure of the underworld. He had started out as a mortal whose knowledge of agriculture and wine-making made him a much beloved figure throughout Egypt. However, this popularity made Seth so jealous that he became singularly focused on killing off Big Bro. The roundabout murder plan Seth came up with was worthy of history's greatest archfiends: He threw a great big party, at which he offered an unusual door prize—a custom-built sarcophagus. Apparently, handing out a coffin at a party back then was not the downer it might be today, and guests vied enthusiastically for the fancy box. The catch, Seth announced, was that the sarcophagus would go only to the person who fit perfectly inside it. (If he had had a Snidely Whiplash mustache, he would have wickedly twirled it at this point, for he had custom built the coffin so that only Osiris would fit inside.) When Osiris laid down in the coffin and found it to be just his size, Seth and a few of his cronies slammed the cover down, sealed it shut, and tossed it into the Nile. Osiris drowned.

But before Seth could enjoy life as an only child, Osiris's wife Isis used some magic spells to bring her husband back to life. Enraged, Seth went a-murderin' again, this time with the decidedly less nuanced approach of carving Osiris into tiny bits and hiding the pieces all over Egypt. But Osiris came back to life again after Isis, with a great deal of wifely devotion, methodically pieced her husband back together, though she couldn't quite ever track down his penis (Honey, the good news is you're alive. The bad news is . . .). Before Osiris could be slaughtered again, a council of gods decided to make the still popular but now memberless Osiris ruler of the underworld, king of the dead.

The son of Osiris and Isis, Horus, was understandably upset with what Uncle Seth had done to his family, and he set out to avenge his dad. Horus engaged Seth in a bloody battle during which he lost an eye and Seth, somewhat fittingly, lost his testicles. Again the other gods stepped in, this time making Horus a king and banishing Seth to oversee the chaos and confusion of the desert.

Seth is an important pre-Satan figure, particularly in appearance. He's often referred to as having the head of a jackal, but he really looks like something out of a mutant aardvark family, with small square ears, long tail, and a large curved snout. In later, Christian devils, that snout became a prominent hooked nose, a feature that blended medieval anti-Semitism with Seth's association as an agent of "foreign threats."

One nondevilish twist in Seth's makeup was that he was not entirely horrible. For all the fratricidal impulses he indulged and all the devastating sandstorms he unleashed, he was still the guy who was trusted to protect sun god Ra as he worked his way through the underworld each night.

PAINFUL BRIDGEWORK

Sixth-century B.C. Persian philosophers such as Zoroaster began to popularize the notion that the universe was a battleground for the ever-clashing forces of good and evil, and that the very qualities of good and evil were mutually exclusive. A divine being could not commit acts of evil, and devilish evildoers had no glimmer of goodness within them. Zoroaster posited the notion that humans could follow the path of one of two spirits: the path of Ahriman, spirit of chaos and destruction, who sought to defile all of creation, or that of Ahura Mazda, the spirit of virtue, who sought above all to remain righteous.

Persians believed that a human's life would be judged on which spirit's path had been followed, and that judgment would be made by Rashnu, the god of the dead.

As he added up a soul's life, it was Rashnu who would command the soul to walk across a narrow bridge (Chinvato Peretu). If the soul had led a virtuous life, that bridge would lead straight to heaven, and as a bonus, the soul would be accompanied by a fetching young nubile. But if the soul had lived a wicked and licentious life, the bridge would become narrower and narrower as they walked, until it was like the edge of a razor, at which point the soul would tumble into an awful abyss to be consumed by hungry, teeth-gnashing demons at the command of Yima, the first man to die.

While Rashnu was in the position to condemn and

punish souls, he, unlike so many other lords of the dead, took no pleasure from it and was considered to be of unimpeachable virtue himself. But Ahriman, sometimes known as Angra Mainya, delighted in watching souls tumble to hell. He was the source of all evil and darkness in the world, who had consciously chosen to be a wicked soul rather than to worship the goodness that his twin spirit Ahura Mazda had created. For Persian believers, it was Ahriman who was constantly trying to ruin the good days that Ahura Mazda sent their way. He was the devil who created excessive cold in the winter, excessive heat in the summer, and disease and pestilence all year long. It was also believed that one of Ahriman's most powerful weapons was his ability to inflame the passions and induce mind-warping lust. Those who couldn't hold out for the heavenly nubiles were sure to be tumbled off the razor bridge by the weight of their own engorged desires.

If Ahriman had a particularly bitter edge to him, it was because he knew he was fighting a losing battle. He was well aware that in the period preceding the cosmic cataclysm at the end of the world, he would be granted a brief period of semivictory by Ahura Mazda, but would eventually be defeated by his twin's forces of goodness, and would in fact be annihilated.

DEVIL-FREE ZONING

In November 2001, Carolyn Risher, the mayor of the small town of Inglis, Florida, saw fit to take a proactive measure against evil. By official mayoral proclamation she banned Satan from stepping within Inglis city limits. According to a *St. Petersburg Times* article by Alex Leary, that document read: "Be it known from this day forward that Satan, ruler of darkness, giver of evil, destroyer of what is good and just, is not now, nor ever again will be, a part of this town of Inglis. Satan is hereby declared powerless, no longer ruling over, nor influencing, our citizens." Copies of the proclamation were placed inside hollowed-out wooden posts at the four entrances to town.

Satan himself has not been spotted near Inglis since, but the wooden posts were stolen shortly after they went up. The mayor then planned to replace them with larger posts set in reinforced concrete.

One particularly powerful Hindu goddess occasionally displays a devilish temperament and has sometimes been misperceived as a devil: Kali, the fierce, unpredictable warrior aspect of the mother goddess Devi. Kali first appears by springing forth from the goddess Durga to help do away with a phalanx of demons that are wreaking havoc in heaven and on earth, and the heat of battle transforms her into a being capable of formidable carnage. She is not a figure of evil, though—in fact, she resolutely protects her followers against evil spirits. But she is nonetheless a fearsome sight. In paintings and tapestries, Kali is usually pictured in battle-ready state: She has angry, piercing eyes, her bloodred tongue protrudes from her mouth, and she uses her many arms (usually four, sometimes more) to grasp a severed head, a sword, and, in some depictions, a holy book, a string of prayer beads, a bowl of blood, and additional weaponry. She wears a not-so-flattering skirt made of bits of slain demon foes, and she is almost always accessorized with a necklace of vanquished demon skulls, a belt of severed arms, and earrings fashioned from demon parts.

She has a frightening countenance, but Kali is loved and respected as a goddess overseeing the cycle of life and death (hubby Shiva serves as a powerful god of destruction in that cycle), and her arms are capable of both protective, life-affirming power as well as deadly force. Kali also represents an intriguing mixture of symbols of motherhood and mortality. As fearsome a creature as she is, she significantly is also often depicted as a full-breasted woman who, in the act of motherhood, creates both life and, by logical extension, death (sometimes her earrings are made of dead children).

Kali is often portrayed standing with one foot atop the prone Shiva, with sword held high. But in other images of the goddess, she dances with wild abandon, often surrounded by subordinate spirits. Some Kali devotees believe that the wilder Kali's dance becomes, the more powerful (and unpredictable) the goddess becomes.

BOTHERING BUDDHA

Mara was a Hindu demon who was eventually appropriated by some sects of Buddhism to become a ruler of the underworld. His role in the religion was not so much as a tormentor of men, living or dead, but as an annoyer of the Buddha. Mara was forever trying to tempt the

Buddha from his ascetic ways and to knock him off the path to enlightenment. Mara's devilish distractions included a trio of attractive daughters who danced suggestively before the Buddha and attempted to seduce him; an army of demons who attempted to startle and frighten the Buddha; and a handful of lightning bolts thrown straight at the Buddha's head. None of it worked. The Buddha remained focused and attained enlightenment. Mara sulked.

ME SO HORNED

The roots of the appearance and behavior of the modern devil stretch back through ancient Hebrew beliefs to those of the Canaanites. The Canaanites worshipped Moloch, who was envisioned as a wrathful old man with horns, those horns being a visual detail that would mark many devils to come. Moloch also was an early advocate of fiery doom; he commanded that children be sacrificed to him, and preferred that they be burned (it was at a temple to Moloch that sacrifices were carried out in the valley of Hinnom, or Gehenna).

Moloch's horns and temperament have also had an impact on the world of reptiles. One of the most arrestingly bizarre members of the lizard world is a multiple-horned Australian native, the thorny devil or mountain devil. The Latin name for the creature is *Moloch horridus*.

YOUR GOD STINKS

"Beelzebub" is a devil name sometimes used inter-changeably with "Satan." The name turns up in the Bible as a reference to a pagan god (2 Kings 1:2). An alternate form, Beelzebul, shows up in the Gospels of Matthew, Mark, and Luke as a powerful demon (except in King James translations, where there's only Beelzebub). Eventually, among medieval Christians both names became widely used either as aliases for Satan or as names of key demons. John Milton made Beelzebub Satan's second-in-command in *Paradise Lost*.

The names actually stem from a bit of interreligious put-down. Baal was a god of fertility to ancient Phoenicians and Canaanites, and that name was also used as a general title of "lord" for the gods of many Semitic cultures. Jewish believers, wishing to disparage the idol worship around them, came up with a tongue-tripping show of disrespect for Baal, linking the god's name to their words for flies, *zebub*, or excrement, *zebul*. Thus, a swipe at somebody else's god created Beelzebub and Beelzebul, respectively, the lord of the flies and—not to put too fine a point on it—the lord of crap.

PLEASE ALLOW HIM TO INTRODUCE HIMSELF

The concert held at the Altamont Speedway outside of San Francisco on December 6, 1969, is rightfully considered one of the worst events in rock 'n' roll history. Despite a promising lineup of Santana, the Flying Burrito Brothers, the Grateful Dead, Jefferson Airplane, the Rolling Stones, and Crosby, Stills, Nash and Young, poor planning, bad sound, overcrowding, and less-than-secure security by the Hell's Angels (who were paid in beer) all marred the day. As a result, the Grateful Dead, who were spooked by the mounting bad vibes, split before performing. The day's ugliness reached its nadir with the midconcert stabbing murder of young attendee Meredith Hunter. However, contrary to popular legend that has sprung up around Altamont, the killing did not take place while the Rolling Stones performed

181

> "Sympathy for the Devil." The violence that claimed Hunter's life erupted during "Under My Thumb."

DEVILS' DEVILS: SATAN AND SHAYTAN

We come to the devil's most freighted, weighted, and worrisome title: Satan. The name springs from a much less grandiose word, the uncapitalized *satan*, which in ancient Hebrew simply referred to an enemy, one of human rather than supernatural scale. This form of the word appears often in Hebrew scripture to describe any number of adversaries or members of opposition forces, and it occasionally refers to spirits in heaven who may disagree with decisions that God has made. As the Israelites did not have a very strong concept of a hell of damnation, they had no need for a cosmically evil leader of a netherworld, so the idea of "satan" did not achieve singular, proper-noun status.

Islam gave a prominent role to the devil, who was depicted as the persistent tempter of men, and who, from

Arabic etymological roots, was identified as Shaytan or Shaitan. Much as in Christian theology, Shaytan was said to be a fallen spirit who had been cast out of heaven by Allah because he demonstrated pride and arrogance. Before the fall, Shaytan is known as Iblis, and is not an angel but a djinn, a spirit creature made from fire. When Allah asks his angels and Iblis to bow before his creation, Adam, Iblis refuses. Iblis tells Allah he won't do it because he, being made of fire, is better than Adam, who is made of mud. This gets him cast down hellward, with one small proviso: While Iblis (Shaytan) will have no power over Allah or his devout followers, he is free to tempt humanity toward sinfulness.

Satan, in the guise of the serpent in the Garden of Eden, is the tempter who initiates the Fall of Man into sinfulness. But throughout much of the Old Testament, Satan is more an inchoate notion of wickedness rather than a figure of ultimate evil. It is in the later texts of the Bible, particularly in the Gospels and the book of Revelation, that Satan is recognized as a very vivid arch-enemy of God and Jesus Christ. In Revelation, Satan's presence is eventually extended with the introduction of the ultimate, human embodiment of living evil, the false prophet, or Antichrist.

A further word on that serpent in the Garden of Eden. The temptation of Eve and the Fall of Man have been placed squarely on the shoulderless body of that devilish snake through centuries of literature, artwork, and sermonizing, but in scripture he is not immediately identified as Satan. The serpent is introduced as "more subtil than any beast of the field" (Gen. 3:1), "subtil" meaning crafty, cunning, or shrewd. He does not identify himself, and in fact the term "Satan" is not used at all in Genesis—though in Revelation, Satan is referred to as "that old serpent" (Rev. 12:19, 20:2).

The serpent's trickery is a matter of twisting meaning. God's very first words to Adam had been the command not to eat of the tree of knowledge, warning, "In the day that thou eatest thereof, thou shalt surely die" (Gen. 2:7), a warning that death will become a part of human existence. The serpent tells Eve that she won't die—not in the sense of dropping dead immediately—but that "your eyes shall be opened and ye shall be as gods, knowing good and evil" (Gen. 3:5). And with that bit of obfuscation, the Fall of Man is put into motion. (In Milton's *Paradise Lost*, the serpent's pitch to Eve is a bit more extended, and he cunningly makes use of what sounds like an evenhanded and logical argument.)

In medieval paintings and stained glass, the serpent was often given a more active role, pictured wrapped around the tree of knowledge or even handing Eve the fruit. The serpent was sometimes portrayed as having the devil's head and upper body. As for the fruit itself, tradition holds that it was an apple, but nowhere in Genesis is it so identified.

CURSED

When God sees what has happened in the Garden of Eden, Eve quickly blames the snake for her transgression, and God in turn curses the serpent by pronouncing, "[U]pon thy belly shalt thou go, and dust shalt thou eat all the days of thy life" (Gen. 3:4). This has raised an interesting question for Bible scholars: How was the serpent getting around before the curse? Some have suggested that he had legs prior to the curse, while others raise the possibility he was able to move about in an upright fashion (in many of those medieval paintings and stained-glass windows, the serpent is upright on just one small coil of tail). A minority viewpoint has suggested that the serpent may have at first been winged, while a more common view holds that the curse did not change the serpent's form, but condemned him to continue to crawl on his belly, now in a degraded state (not only is he eating dust, but he is "cursed above every beast of the field" (Gen. 3:14)).

TALKER

One key piece of evidence cited to prove that the serpent in Genesis is Satan is that he speaks. The serpent is one of two talking animals in the Old Testament, the other being a donkey in the book of Numbers commonly referred to as "Balaam's ass." But the serpent is the only one that speaks for himself. In the case of the donkey, it is God speaking through the animal, pointing out to Balaam the fact that Balaam has become violently angry because the ass would not follow his commands, when Balaam himself has not followed the Lord's commands.

URGE OVERKILL

A few belief systems dispense with the idea of the devil, instead teaching of a Demiurge, a force that created all that is physical and worldly (as opposed to all that's spiritual and celestial). The word originally referred to a craftsman—one who built things for public use, but came to refer to the masterworker who had put the universe together. Greek philosopher Plato considered the Demiurge to be a benevolent force, although some flaws in its nature allowed for chaos and wickedness in the world. In some Gnostic beliefs, the materialistic and sensuous Demiurge is a bit more devilish, and serves as an active force of opposition to the Supreme Creator of the celestial realm.

OH GOD, YOU DEVIL

Those Gnostic Cathars of twelfth-century France seem to have been willing to make their way peacefully through their concept of earth as hell, but their unorthodox beliefs in other regards made them the target of widespread heresy charges. Chiefly, they were assailed for their belief that the God of the Old Testament, having created the evil of the world, was the figure of ultimate evil. The Old Testament God was, in effect, the Cathar Satan. The Christian church was not willing to let such beliefs stand.

In 1209, Pope Innocent III launched a particularly bloody, decades-long Crusade against the Cathars. Thousands of Cathars were slaughtered as heretics and blasphemers and sent, in the eyes of the crusaders, to the fiery, eternal subterranean hell they had not believed in.

HELL'S FISHWICH

- Satan is also the name of a genus of catfish (*Satan eurystomus*).
- Devilfish are a species of huge manta ray that can measure twenty feet across and weigh a ton. Despite their scary-as-hell appearance, they eat only plankton and have been known to frolic with intrepid swimmers.

GET A JOB

Aside from the ultimate showdown of the Apocalypse, one of the Bible's most direct confrontations between God and Satan can be found in the Old Testament book of Job. The story of Job is an attempt to wrestle with the problem of evil—i.e., how can bad things happen in a world created by an all-powerful, benevolent God; are the bad things that happen always intended as a punishment; and how are humans supposed to endure and survive their suffering? In the story of Job, Satan doesn't yet appear to be the embodiment of all evil. In the King James Version he's described as one of the "sons of God," and he and God actually seem to have a cordial, conversational relationship (early in the book, God asks Satan where he has been, and Satan replies that he has been walking about on the earth). Rather than acting as lord of darkness, Satan takes on more the role of an adversarial peanut gallery, lobbing pesky questions and challenges at God.

When God shows some obvious pride and pleasure in the devotion of Job, a wealthy and righteous family man, the crafty Satan raises a bit of a problematic, spiritual question. He suggests that Job is a faithful servant of the Lord because he has a materially good life, but that if he did not live so well, he would not have such powerful faith. Satan wagers that if God were to test Job with some bad times, the rich man would end up cursing God rather than worshipping him.

Somewhat uncharacteristically, God accepts Satan's little wager. He will allow Satan to rain down catastrophes upon Job, as long as Job is not physically harmed. Satan jumps to the task enthusiastically, and in a day Job loses all his material wealth, and has his family destroyed by a deadly windstorm that collapses their house. But Job does not curse God. Satan asks if he can up the punishment a bit, and again God agrees, with the stipulation that Job not be killed. Satan has Job covered with boils from head to toe and reduces him to an abject, wretched state. Job never curses God, but after a long conversation with some less-than-supportive old friends, he finally does question his fate and God's motives. God appears to Job, and eventually Job repents of his moments of doubt and renews his vows of faith to God. God in turn gives Job twice as much wealth as he had before, and a new, very attractive family. God also has some harsh words for Job's so-called friends, but he does not discipline Satan for his role in Job's suffering.

One conclusion that can be drawn from Job's tale: Satan can do some terrible things to mortals, but only if God—the more powerful force—allows it.

HERE'S LUCIFER

Early Christians came to believe that Satan, prior to his banishment from heaven, existed as an archangel named Lucifer. That name, from a Latin phrase meaning "light bearer," was sometimes used in Latin translations of the book of Isaiah in the Hebrew Bible as part of the phrase "brilliant one, son of the morning" (in the King James Bible, Isaiah 14:12 refers to "Lucifer, son of the morning"). Lucifer is never expressly identified as Satan, and the details of his fall are never made explicitly clear. But, in the Middle Ages, the name was accepted as a way of referring to Satan in his pre-Fall state. The name gained even wider acceptance with the publication in 1667 of John Milton's *Paradise Lost.* With that epic poem, Milton followed in what had been a decades-old trend of plays and poems centered on the devil's fall from grace. Milton, in beautifully memorable language, established what would become many of the conventions of the Western understanding of the devil: his haughty pride, his perverse pleasure in his banishment, his gleeful attempts to grab hold of human souls. And in a pre-Jagger/Richards example of sympathy for the devil, Milton's fallen Lucifer, embracing his new role as Satan with antihero relish, vented spleen in a phrase that many indignant, downtrodden mortals might very well relate to: "Better to reign in hell than serve in heaven."

MY HELL

JOHN RECHY

Novelist: *City of Night, The Life and Adventures of Lyle Clemens*

Hell is the opposite of Heaven.

So what is Heaven?

A place where feathery angels and chubby cherubs gambol on puffy clouds while singing the praises of the Celestial Dictator?

That's what Lucifer, the first rebel, could not tolerate; and so he and other angelic rebels were tossed out of Heaven and into Hell by His Celestial Petulance.

So what is Hell?

A place of adventurous rebellion, eternal questioning.

Do evil miscreants find their place among the righteous outlaws?

Heavens, no.

They would have, with all their earthly cunning intact, squirmed their way into Heaven, gaining favor with their fellow Tyrant.

IMAGE IS EVERYTHING

In the first centuries of the Christian church, the devil was still often considered in terms of his status as a fallen angel, and was sometimes portrayed with his wings and halo still intact. It was during the Middle Ages that paintings, woodcuts, and lithographs of Satan began to turn him into a more monstrous form, mixing the looks of the Canaanite Moloch, the pagan Pan, and other unseemly spirits to portray him as a Satyr-like monster with cloven hooves, horns, and a tail. It was this imagery that gained popular acceptance as the devil shifted from a mysterious figure of the scriptures into one of ultimate evil easily recognized by the culture-at-large.

During the Middle Ages, throughout Europe the devil made a gradual shift from a figure of strictly religious significance to one more intimately tied to the day-to-day, earthbound existence of humans (and perhaps their hellbound demise). The horned, hooved, often leering Satan began to turn up in all sorts of popular entertainments, including parades, plays, festivals, puppet shows, and semipornographic hell-related pamphlets that offered up equal helpings of fiery sermonizing and calculated titillation. In these presentations the devil began to display a sense of wicked humor, using his cunning to tempt and entice vulnerable humans into actions that would lead to their descent into hell. Devil tales offered a way to make scenes of lewd and lusty behavior acceptable to a public audience, for the lubricious sinners were, after all, going to be punished by story's end for their carnal sins. Such tales also offered a bit of satisfying class consciousness: The devil often brought about a delicious comeuppance to haughty, self-important figures of wealth, authority, and outright wickedness, with members of the clergy frequently turning up in one of these categories. (He's still doing some of the same work on hell-based episodes of *South Park*.)

YOU CAN CALL ME . . .

Nicknames for the devil include: Old Scratch, Old Nick, Old Horny, Black Jack, Lusty Dick, the Baker, the Stoker, the Tempter, the Old

Gentleman, the Beast, the Serpent, the Deceiver, the God of This World, the Father of All Lies, and the Prince of Darkness.

ANTICHRIST

The term "Antichrist" shows up in the Bible in John's Epistles (1 John 2:22, 2 John 1:7). There it refers to false prophets and to those who would deny that Jesus is the Messiah. The Antichrist rises to his full powers within the apocalyptic visions of the book of Revelation, where he is assumed to be the figure described as the "beast" or the "false prophet." Some interpretations view the Antichrist as a potent, cunning ambassador from hell, ruling the earth during a period of trials and tribulations before the return of Christ. As the "beast," he is described as a monstrous creature with ten horns and seven heads, but most prophetic interpretations of Revelation hold that the Antichrist will begin his reign in human form as a very popular, gravely deceptive world leader. When the Last Judgment takes place, the Antichrist and all his followers (identifiable because they bear his mark) will be cast into "the lake of fire."

GOT HIS NUMBER

Within the apocalyptic turmoil of the book of Revelation is a bit of hellish numerics that has resonated across the centuries: the number "666," which according to author John in some way identifies the Antichrist.

Experts have not been able to convincingly decode the meaning of 666. In popular devil mythology, the number has come to refer to a literal mark of the beast— it actually appears on the flesh of the Antichrist. But some Bible scholars believe the numbers may refer to the Roman emperor Nero. According to a system of assigning numerical values to Hebrew letters that was used by early Christians, when "Caesar Nero" ("King Nero") is written in Hebrew and then added up, it totals 666.

"Six" is significant because in some systems of numerology, it was considered an imperfect number, one short of the perfect seven. Revelation also includes plenty of sevens, including seven churches, seven seals, seven trumpets, seven angels, and seven bowls of the wrath of God.

BIG FEET, BIG PRINTS

On the night of February 8, 1855, a heavy, hours-long snowfall blanketed the countryside of south Devon in England. The next morning, early risers in the many villages of Devon were surprised to find strange, hooflike track marks in the snow, running through streets, around buildings, across farmland, and through the open hillsides. The tracks, resembling footprints from some large bipedal creature, stretched for over a hundred miles through Devon, and seemed to continue unimpeded over roofs and through walls, fences, and other obstructions, as if the barriers simply weren't there. Word spread from town to town, and soon the magnitude of the phenomenon left locals with only one feasible explanation: The marks were the footprints of the devil. Naturalists were called out to examine the tracks, and the phenomenon was reported widely in the national press. Quoth the *London Times*: "Considerable sensation has been evoked in the towns of Topsham, Lympstone, Exmouth, Teignmouth and Dawlish, in the south of Devon, in consequence of the discovery of a vast number of foot-tracks of a most strange and mysterious description. The superstitious go so far as to believe that they are the marks of Satan himself."

The scientific community struggled to come up with an alternative explanation that would account for so many tracks across so wide an area. Theories that were floated attributed the tracks to badgers, raccoons, otters, swans, escaped kangaroos, and a hot air balloon dragging a rope. But no reasonable explanation held up. To this day, the case of the devil's footprints remains as much a mystery as it was back in 1855.

BIG HOOVES, BIG . . .

In medieval art and legend, Satan started to become less a direct adversary of God and more a tempter of individual men and women. Particularly women. As the witchcraft craze of the twelfth century began to heat up, it was said that Satan took a personal interest both in recruiting witches and in attending their purportedly orgiastic sabbats.

From the confessions of those accused of witchcraft (notoriously unreliable as they were almost always obtained by means of torture) and the writings of witchhunters, a highly detailed, exceedingly erotic picture of the devil began to emerge (as was the case with some apocalyptic tracts, ostensibly pious work allowed for the most prurient of discussions).

The devil's preferred method of recruiting women was to appear before them, seduce them, and then take the form of an animal in order to copulate with them (he-goats, bulls, stags, dogs, and mules seem to have been favorites). After that nasty act, the woman was in the devil's service.

At the witches' sabbats, the devil often skipped the animal transformation and had intercourse with women while in his true demonic form. His genitals were said to be enormous, but telling details differed: Sometimes they were said to be perfectly proportioned, even handsome; sometimes they were described as scaly and frightening; several confessions described a spiked or double-pronged penis.

The women's experience of devil encounters varied as well. Sometimes the sex was said to be so pleasurable that the devil's partner remained in a kind of trance for days. Other times, the copulation was described as being as painful as childbirth. One odd detail shows up in many descriptions: The devil's semen is ice-cold.

Witches' sabbats were said to conclude with one final act of sexual degradation, the "osculum infame" (roughly, "dirty kiss"), during which the witch planted a smooch on an unspeakable region of the devil's nether quarters.

DEVIL, BE GONE

In the 1985 porno film *New Wave Hookers*, the devil was portrayed in fleshily accommodating fashion by erstwhile porn star Traci Lords. Shortly after the film's release, it was discovered that Lords had been under the age of consent during filming. When the film was rereleased on video and DVD during the 1990s, the devil's sex scenes had been edited out.

DESPERATE HOUSEWITCHES

Why were women considered to be so vulnerable to the erotic entreaties of Satan? Two chief witch-hunters of the church's Inquisition, Heinrich Kramer and Jacob Sprenger, wrote in their encyclopedic witch-finding guide *Malleus Maleficarum* that women, due to their sexed-up nature, just couldn't help but fornicate with the devil: "All witchcraft comes from carnal lust, which in women is insatiable. . . . Wherefore for the sake of fulfilling their lusts they consort even with devils. Much more reasons could be brought forward, but to the understanding it is sufficiently clear that it is no matter for wonder that there are more women than men found infected with the heresy of witchcraft."

UNSEXY DEVIL

The devil was sometimes believed to be hindering sex rather than initiating it. Thirteenth-century theologian Thomas Aquinas, in his *Quodlibet XI*, proposed that the work of God is stronger than the work of the devil. However, Aquinas pointed out that although the devil and holy matrimony were both works of God, the devil was slightly more powerful than matrimony. Thus, the devil would do what he could to impede marriage by means of sexual impotence, causing holy unions to either fail or go unconsummated.

IS THERE A DOCTOR IN THE HOUSE?

Out of medieval devil stories grew one of the devil's most famous literary incarnations, that of Mephistopheles, the devil of the Faust legend. In the story, Doctor Faust—sometimes written as Faustus—has a hunger for supernatural or forbidden knowledge, and through a bit of less-than-expert haggling, exchanges his soul's eternal damnation for a couple of decades of wealth and success. There are some records of a real Doctor Faustus living in Germany in the early 1500s. He studied medicine, sorcery, astrology, and alchemy, picking up a reputation as a dangerous quack along the way and finding himself run out of more than a few towns when his purported cures led to further ailments.

From whatever the doctor's real acts of quackery may have been, a body of folk legends began to grow around his name. Increasingly dramatic, openly fictional tales of the adventures of Doctor Faustus circulated for years, and were given notable form when Christopher Marlowe drew upon the legends to create his play *The Tragical History of Doctor Faustus* in 1590. Two hundred years later, the legend still had power with the public, and Goethe further refined it in his play *Faust*. The primary devil in these works is Mephistopheles (Marlowe called him Mephistophilis), a right-hand man to the all-powerful Satan, who answers Faust's summons and brokers the deal for his soul. Mephistopheles is a significant figure in devil history because he marks a departure from the devil as either a rampant creature of carnal hungers or a conniving, master tempter. He is, instead, a serious and almost somber character who, far from being horned and hoofed, has the appearance of a sophisticated gentleman. Mephistopheles in no way is out to trick Faust; in fact, he is quite open about how unpleasant eternal damnation will be, and he takes pains to make sure that Faust completely understands what he is getting into. This shift in the devil's personality makes the moral of the Faust tales more an indictment of human nature than of insidious deviltry. It is Faust's own hubris and self-regard, not the devil's trickery, that sends his soul hellward.

TAZ

The Tasmanian devil is the world's largest carnivorous marsupial. Early European settlers of the Australian island of Tasmania named this squat, nocturnal creature "the devil" due to its thick black fur, aggressive temperament, and ability to unleash pants-soiling screeches. In animated form, the Tasmanian devil was a featured costar in several classic Looney Tunes cartoons.

DON'T CROSS AT THE CORNER

The Faustian bargain lives on in such modern entertainments as the musical *Damn Yankees* and the film *Bedazzled*. It also echoed in the "crossroads" mythology of American blues music, which is probably best embodied by the legend surrounding early bluesman Robert Johnson.

Johnson, born in Mississippi in 1911, grew up living the hard life of a migrant worker in cotton fields. But he showed an early aptitude for music, and by the time he was a teenager, he was playing guitar and writing songs, and was soon making a living playing the juke joints of the Deep South. In 1930, his teenage wife died in childbirth, and their baby died shortly thereafter. The legend holds that Johnson, despondent and angry with God, went one midnight to the crossroads of Highways 61 and 49 in Clarksdale, Mississippi. He called upon the devil to appear, and when Satan showed up, Johnson struck a deal: If the devil would tune Johnson's guitar, thus granting him supernatural musical abilities, the devil could lay claim to Johnson's soul.

For a while the deal worked in Johnson's favor. He was widely respected as a master of his craft and was one of the few bluesmen to be recorded, allegedly being paid a top fee of ten dollars a song. This allowed his music to be heard outside of live appearances and to travel more widely than he did. But apparently the devil resented Johnson's success, because in August 1938, Johnson took a slug from an open whiskey bottle in a saloon and promptly went into terrible convulsions (some accounts say he was poisoned by the boyfriend of a woman Johnson had his eye on). He died a few days later.

The Johnson legend is fueled by the Johnson tune "Crossroads," and some believe it is the song itself that is cursed. Eric Clapton, the Allman Brothers, and Lynyrd Skynyrd all recorded it and all later suffered career-altering tragedies.

A Johnson-like figure finally got a bit of devilish revenge with the Charlie Daniels Band's 1979 hit, "The Devil Went Down to Georgia." In that tune, a fleet-fingered bumpkin named Johnny manages to save his soul by outfiddling the Dark One.

JOIZY BOY

If a devil can't skulk about the pits and caverns of hell itself, perhaps the marshlands of New Jersey are an acceptable second best.

For over 260 years, stories have been told of a strange, possibly demonic creature that stalks the Pine Barrens of the Garden State, the Jersey Devil.

The ecologically unique Pine Barrens are spread over a million acres of southeastern New Jersey and include farms, forests, suburbs, and wetlands. Huge undeveloped stretches of the area are home to such natural oddities as pygmy forests, orchid bogs, and cedar swamps that stain nearby streams blood red with the tannin of the trees. During colonial times, these swamps were a significant impediment to travel, and only a few Indian trails and traders' roads wound their way through the shadowy quiet of the unsettled barrens.

There are several different versions of the origin of the Jersey Devil, but the most-told seem to center either on a woman living in the town of Leeds Point or a woman whose name was Leeds. In 1735, this woman, who may or may not have been a sorceress, gave birth to her thirteenth child— a terribly deformed creature whose twisted body was marked with winglike appendages, a not-so-vestigial tail, and hooflike feet. The child was strictly confined to the Leeds home at first, but as soon as he was able, he escaped (in various tellings, either through the cellar or, more dramatically, up the chimney). The creature dashed off into the barrens, where he developed strange powers that many locals cited as the cause behind crop failures, gory livestock deaths, family illnesses, and just about any natural disaster (or inconvenience).

The Jersey Devil ostensibly sought solitude and privacy, but as he continued to dash about the barrens he was sometimes glimpsed by some very surprised witnesses. Documented sightings began turning up in the 1800s. It was claimed that American naval hero Commodore Stephen Decatur had spotted the devil flying through the air near Browns Mills, New Jersey, while the commodore was testing cannonballs for the brewing War of 1812. Joseph Bonaparte, Napoleon's brother and a former king of Naples and of Spain, lived for fifteen years in a New Jersey estate called Point Breeze, and stories claimed that while out on a hunting expedition, Bonaparte had spotted the devil disappearing into some woods near Bordentown.

The devil's geographic range slowly continued to expand, until he apparently grew tired of the secluded life, and in one week in January 1909, he revealed himself to over a thousand people, from the tip of South Jersey right up through Philadelphia, Camden, and Trenton, and on up to the New York State border. Most witnesses described a birdlike or winged creature with the head of a doglike horse or a horselike dog. The creature was hideous to look at, but it didn't seem to present much of a mortal threat—its main response to human contact seems to have been shrieking horribly and flying away.

The 1909 sightings were written up extensively in newspapers of the day, which elevated the devil from a bit of dark local lore to an official, celebrated folk legend. The Jersey Devil has continued to reveal himself over the years, sticking to his traditional modus operandi of appearing suddenly, shrieking horribly, and then retreating.

The creature was paid indisputable tribute in 1982 when Jersey's NHL hockey franchise was named the New Jersey Devils. The Devils have won five division championships, four conference championships, and three Stanley Cups, primarily by playing a strong defensive game—and perhaps by shrieking horribly at opponents.

NO SYMPATHY HERE

The sizable sand dunes of Kill Devil Hills, North Carolina, were the site of the Wright brothers first aircraft flight in 1903 (Orville Wright telegraphed news of the success from the nearby, and more familiar, Kitty Hawk). The place may have gotten its name from the barrels of god-awful Kill Devil liquor that occasionally tumbled off colonial-era rumrunners' boats and washed ashore there.

PULP FRICTION

Works of modern literature, from *The Wizard of Oz* to the Harry Potter series, have been banned by American school boards for supposed hints of occultism and satanism. But over the years a couple of openly devilish works have slipped into American comic-book racks without raising much fuss. Captain Satan was a line of comics published in the late 1930s whose title character was a very mortal but darkly nicknamed detective—"King of Detectives," as his subtitle would have it.

More devilishly, in 1957, Harvey Comics followed up its success with Casper the Friendly Ghost by unleashing Hot Stuff, who was essentially a tiny, mischievous, cute-as-a-button Prince of Darkness sporting both diaper and pitchfork.

The titles did not demonstrate any great degree of

satanic power. After five issues, Captain Satan was retooled and retitled Strange Detective Stories. Harvey Comics ceased publishing in 1982.

MY HELL

JOHN KRICFALUSI

Animator, director, creator of "Ren and Stimpy"

I feel like I live through a little piece of hell every time I go to the movies. The theatergoing experience is absolutely horrible, and is always getting worse. It's expensive, you have to sit through awful commercials for lousy movies, and then you get the feature you came for, which turns out to be a poorly projected even lousier movie. I would predict that in the afterlife you'll line up for three hours, pay thirty dollars, walk into the theater, and a huge naked fat man will slap you hard in the face and boot you right back out. And you'll have to get back in line again, with everybody muttering, "Yes, this is hell."

I TAWT I TAW A PWINCE OF DAWKNESS . . .

One of the strangest episodes in the eternal struggle between the Looney Tunes forces of Sylvester and Tweety Bird can be found in the 1954 episode "Satan's Waitin'." In this cartoon, Sylvester follows the little bird to the top of a skyscraper, lunges after him, and promptly plunges to the sidewalk below. Upon impact, one of the cat's nine lives descends to hell, which in the Looney Tunes cosmos is overseen by a Satan who looks like a bulldog (Mel Blanc voices bird, cat, and dog). The devil dog reminds Sylvester that he's got eight more lives to make use of, and insists that he continue his pursuit of the elusive Tweety. With Satan's encouragement, Sylvester goes on the hunt again, and proceeds to lose the rest of his lives by means of guns, steamrollers, and carnival mishaps. Tweety remains uneaten.

SEE YOU IN CHURCH

In the summer of 1966, part-time musician, carny, and occult lecturer Anton Szandor LaVey was granted an official charter from the State of California to found and run his own church, the Church of Satan. Over the next few years he published his monographs, *The Satanic Bible*, *The Compleat Witch*, and *The Satanic Rituals*. Sometimes known as the Black Pope, LaVey used a canny mix of sex and showmanship to build an international profile for his church, and to attract a sizable group of followers. He and the church were even ranked worthy of a *Time* cover story in June 1972. LaVey died in 1997, but the church lives on.

Though LaVey's followers consider themselves satanists, their Satan has little to do with any Christian or Muslim notion of ultimate evil. The Church of Satan celebrates a pre-Christian notion of Satan, one that is centered on individuality, sensuality, and an aversion to mainstream convention. In LaVey's series of nine Satanic Statements, the church's Satan is said to represent indulgence (rather than abstinence), "vital existence," "undefiled wisdom," "kindness to those who deserve it," vengeance (rather than turning the other cheek), responsibility, man's animal nature, and all of "the so-called sins." The church also states that Satan is the best friend the Christian church has ever had because "he has kept it in business all these years."

The nine satanic sins are listed as stupidity, pretentiousness, solipsism, self-deceit, herd conformity, lack of perspective, forgetfulness of past orthodoxies, counter-productive pride, and lack of aesthetics.

Among the eleven satanic rules of the earth are admonitions not to give opinions or advice unless one is asked; not to tell troubles to others unless one is sure the others want to hear them; not to make sexual advances unless one is "given the mating signal"; and not to harm children.

There's also this rule: "When walking in open territory, bother no one. If someone bothers you, ask him to stop. If he does not stop, destroy him."

Church of Satan satanists do not believe in the existence of a heaven or hell. And the church does not maintain, and hasn't asked for, tax-exempt status.

ENDNOTE: READY FOR THEIR CLOSE-UPS

We've seen that ultimate evil can come in many different shapes and sizes, with a variety of evil talents, but with a singular hunger for mortal souls. And perhaps if the devil's cleverest wile is to convince us that he doesn't exist, his second cleverest wile is to convince us that he's everywhere, in the guise of anybody. Before we move on to meet a few of the devil's hellish helpers, here's a list of just a few of the thespian souls who have given a cinematic face to the devil (or Satan, Lucifer, or Mephistopheles, depending on the screen credits):

George Méliès, *Le Diable au Convent* (1899)
Harry Agar Lyons, *The World, the Flesh and the Devil* (1914)
Jackie Coogan Sr., *The Kid* (1921)
Charles Middleton, *The Devil's Cabaret* (1931)
Captain DeZita, *Glen or Glenda* (1953)
Vincent Price, *The Story of Mankind* (1957)
Mickey Rooney, *The Private Lives of Adam and Eve* (1960)
Lon Chaney Jr., *The Devil's Messenger* (1961)
Christopher Lee, *Katarsis* (1963)
Peter Cook, *Bedazzled* (1967)
Clay Tanner, *Rosemary's Baby* (1968)
John Carradine, *Autopsy of a Ghost* (1968)
Victor Buono, *The Evil* (1978)
John Ritter, *Wholly Moses!* (1980)
Danny Elfman, *The Forbidden Zone* (1980)
Terence Stamp, *The Company of Wolves* (1984)
Jack Nicholson, *The Witches of Eastwick* (1987)
Colleen Dewhurst, *Exorcist III* (1990)
Robert Vaughan, *Witch Academy* (1993)
Al Pacino, *The Devil's Advocate* (1997)
Gabriel Byrne, *End of Days* (1999)

Elizabeth Hurley, *Bedazzled* (2000)

Robert Goulet, *G-Men from Hell* (2000)

Harvey Keitel, *Little Nicky* (2000)

Jennifer Love Hewitt, *The Devil and Daniel Webster* (2001)

Peter Stormare, *Constantine* (2005)

and

Church of Satan head Anton LaVey got a chance to portray Satan himself in *Invocation of My Demon Brother*, a 1969 experimental short by Kenneth Anger, notable for also featuring the Rolling Stones in performance and Manson Family member Bobby Beausoleil in a supporting role as Satan sideman Lucifer.

WHO THE HELL IS THAT?

Hell is other people. —Jean-Paul Sartre

No sin is worth committing unless it's original. —Oscar Wilde

All those souls.

All that torment.

Wherever and however you find it, there's a lot going on in hell.

And no matter how powerful the devil happens to be, history tells us that he can't run the place by himself—or herself.

Across religions and cultures our devils-in-chief have received considerable help from a boggling variety of demons, monsters, and miscellaneous hell spawn. We mortals have had to contend not only with the temptations of a Master Satan and the looming possibility of eternal damnation, but we've also been beset by a full hierarchy of demonic beings and lesser devils who are equally and energetically intent on making our lives—and afterlives—miserable.

Just as there were underworlds before there were hells proper, so too there was a belief in evil spirits and mischievous demigods before there were beliefs in demons per se. In fact, the very term "demon" did not always carry a connotation of frightening evil. The word derives from the Greek *daemon*, which simply means "divine power." In Homer's epic poems, "gods" and "demons" are almost interchangeable terms for supernatural beings. In other legends, "demon" described a being that was classified somewhere between a mortal and a god—either the love child of a human/god get-together, or the result of a particularly worthy human gifted with some godlike powers.

To a large degree, early demons were used to explain the sometimes cruel whims of the natural world, and in doing so such spirits served a crucial role: As personifications of the forces of nature, they connected believers to beliefs on a personal level. The gods of greater power provided stories and explanations of the bigger topics—birth, death, the creation of the universe. However, it was the entities of more limited, but also more observable powers—the spirits and proto demons—

who had a direct effect on any day-to-day life. So, while the average Babylonian field-worker may not have felt he had much of a role in the grand, cosmic goings-on of the greater gods, he could be sure he was receiving plenty of attention from the *utukki*, the demonic spirits that oversaw particularly annoying parts of the earthly world around him. In a time when the march of science had yet to produce much information on encroaching cold fronts or gut-wrangling viruses, it was clearly Idiptu, the wind demon, who blew the roof off the worker's house, and obviously Umma, the fever demon, who kept his baby screaming and vomiting all night.

As the less judgmental underworlds became hells of punishment, the peskier, more mean-spirited spirits were assigned roles there, and eventually—through both church teachings and legend—they became full-fledged demons. Once they were at work down below, demons picked up the responsibility for overseeing particular sins and weaknesses of human flesh. Not only might demons be to blame for making the summer too hot and dry for the crops, they were also behind more personal afflictions, from unquenchable can't-stop-carbo-loading gluttony to chronic can't-keep-my-hands-off-myself masturbation.

There are a couple of notable trends in demon history:

First, like the landscape of hell itself, much of the information about demons has been developed outside of sacred texts and scripture. While demons are certainly present in the Zoroastrian Avesta, the Hebrew Bible, and the New Testament, a semiscience of demonology has always flourished outside of such works, enumerating and describing an often remarkable number of evil spirits at large. Demonologists from medieval times right up to modern times have assembled incredibly detailed demon hierarchies and family trees, often producing end results that rival both the complexity of corporate flowcharts and federal tax codes. Some of these have been collected in "grimoires," books that collect lists of demons along with the spells and incantations necessary to either call forth or subdue each one. The demons themselves might be listed in accordance with their rank in hell, by the extent of their powers, by the sin they were associated with, or even by the month in which they were considered to be dominant. And these could be very extensive works. Many medieval Christian demonologies have seventy-two demonic underlings serving Satan, each of whom commands a multitude of demonic subordinates.

Another important theme in demonology has been that there's no better way to hawk a loogie at another religion than by turning its gods into demons. The old

Sanskrit term *deva* ("to shine") was used to refer to Hindu entities in charge of forces of nature, which were neither good nor evil. But as the term made the jump to Zoroastrianism, devas became *daevas*, rampant evil spirits bent on spreading, disease, degradation, and faithlessness. Hebrew culture demonized Egyptian and Canaanite gods, and Christian demonologists made use of figures drawn from a variety of ancient religions to recruit lesser devils for their visions of hell.

Who are these lesser devils?

Here, we meet a few:

PAIN IN THE ASSYRIANS

In the mountainous region of northern Mesopotamia spread the kingdom of Assyria, which began life in the eighteenth century B.C. as a colony of Babylonia, but eventually rose to become a formidable, mercantile-minded, militarily dominant, colonial power of its own. By the eighth century B.C., Assyrians were brutal Mesopotamian bullies, having conquered and absorbed such Hebrew Bible/Old Testament locales as Judea, Damascus, Samaria, Phoenicia, and Hamath. Those big times lasted about a century, and by 600 B.C. the Assyrian kingdom had collapsed, its rise and fall in striking accord with several biblical prophecies.

The Assyrian bent toward bloody conquest and enslavement led to some oddly linked advances of intellect. The Assyrian's desire to become better warriors resulted in such pioneering developments as iron swords, battle armor, aqueducts, refined medical implements, and the precise application of latitude and longitude (the better to plot out conquered lands). In addition, the Assyrian empire was one of the first vibrant melting pots of history, in which previously secluded and independent city-states found themselves swapping cultures and, to some extent, sharing a common language (referred to in modern times as Akkadian).

Take some Assyrian mathematics, apply to a fertile crescent's worth of gods and demigods, and one result is an extensive, remarkably detailed demonology.

While Assyrian culture had a public and official religion based upon a pantheon of greater gods, evidence on cuneiform tablets, amulets, and various talismans of the time indicates there was a more personal sort of underground religion that recognized a multitude of spirits that impacted constantly and directly on Assyrian lives. These spirits could be contacted or repelled through complicated systems of spells, magic, and sorcery.

The Assyrian demons were understood to reside in the desert, on inaccessible mountaintops, and in the bowels of the earth. Different classes of demon would rise to earth to inflict their own special torment upon a single human, often after using a distinctive point of entry into said human. Alal was a demon of destruction that resided in the chest. Idpa brought fever and entered, logically enough, through the head. The demon of plagues and all-purpose wickedness, Namtar, didn't need a physical grip on a body because it acted on the soul of a person. Sneaking up behind you, Gigim brought weakness through the bowels, while Telal caused the hands to commit acts of violence and thuggery.

Apparently any mortal was under constant and continual threat of demonic possession. Varied incantations were concocted to scat away the assaulting spirits, but even a successful defense one day might not keep that same demon away the next day. And, of course, daytime wasn't really the problem. In the waking hours, prepared Assyrians could make use of all the home-sorcery gear at their disposal to fend off demonic wheedling and needling. But the smarter, nastier demons waited to get at them in the night.

TROUBLE WITH THE EX

The most feared and most insidious of Mesopotamian demons were nocturnal, and included Lilu and his female consort, Lilitu. These two drifted as evil winds across the deserts, and when making contact with humans, they functioned somewhat like sex vampires. They could not only drain a subject of its life force (evidenced by anemia or other wasting illnesses), but they could also wreak havoc with sexual function, fertility, and reproduction. As a result, they were considered particularly perilous to pregnant women. A pair of related demons, Ardat Lili and Idlu Lili, fine-tuned the sex work. *Ardatu* were young girls of marrying age, and Ardat Lili was the spirit that could cause sexual frustration, frigidity, promiscuity, distracting sexual dreams and thoughts, or complete sexual depravity. Ardat Lili's male demonic counterpart, Idlu Lili, was feared as a bringer of impotence.

The bigger demonic point here is that this sexually charged bunch were the collective forebears of a figure who turns up in the Dead Sea Scrolls, the Hebrew Bible, and various apocrypha: Lilith.

In translations of the Hebrew Bible, the name

Lilith was sometimes changed to "great owl"; that's how she turns up in the book of Isaiah, as an owl rather than a woman or she-demon. In the Dead Sea Scrolls, the name is mentioned among a list of demons and owls. But in other texts, especially the medieval epic *The Alphabet of Ben Sira*, the character of Lilith is developed from her demonic predecessors into a human equivalent. It should be pointed out that the *Ben Sira* text is not generally considered to be a work of reliable historical or religious scholarship. In fact, it retells biblical tales in such a highly irreverent fashion that it is sometimes described as an outright work of parody. Nonetheless, Lilith gets a full accounting here. She is Adam's first wife, his mate before Eve was created. (The wiggle room for a first wife comes in Genesis 1:27: "So God created man in his own image, in the image of God created he him; male and female created he them."—This before God creates Eve from Adam's rib in Genesis 2:22).

The *Ben Sira* story holds that Adam and Lilith were a bad match from the start, particularly when it came to the rather crucial matter of sexual compatibility. Adam insisted that since he was the superior being, he should be on top during lovemaking. But Lilith pointed out that since they were both made from dust, they were equal and thus should enjoy each other side by side. Adam asked God to step in and resolve the issue, but Lilith was not interested in any form of compromise or marriage counseling. She instead turned her seductive powers on God himself and, using her formidable feminine wiles, learned his true name, which she promptly shouted to the heavens. As a result, she was banished from Eden (in Judaism, the tetragrammaton, the personal ineffable name of God, is never to be pronounced or read aloud).

Lilith heads off for a demonic rebound romance, energetically mating with the demon Asmodeus (the king of demons in Hebrew lore and apparently a much more cooperative sex partner) and a number of his demon cohorts. When a trio of heavenly angels threatens to kill off Lilith's demonic offspring, she vows to kill the sons of Adam and Eve if she can get to them in their first eight days of life (thus began the Hebrew tradition of placing an amulet bearing angels' names on a male infant before his circumcision).

Asmodeus went on to be recognized as a Christian demon of carnal lust, with a particular interest in fostering homosexuality and destroying new marriages. Lilith went on to become the namesake of a successful women's music festival held in the late 1990s.

How could one fight off the ever-present peril of Mesopotamian demons? Some unique works of pottery found in Babylonian ruins seem to indicate that the answer was simple: Use a bowl. Babylonian demon bowls are covered with inscriptions of antidemon incantations, along with pictures of demons being restrained or depowered. The bowls evidently were used as spirit traps, which could both lure and trap demons before the evil creatures could do any harm. (The demon-ridding rituals could apparently do some damage of their own— some demon bowls have been found to contain fragments of human skull).

MY HELL

PATTON OSWALT
Comic, actor, "enthusiast"

My hell is two days ago. Or two years ago. Or a generation ago. My hell is the good old days, and nostalgia for them.

There were no good old days. No Golden Age. In fact, the term "golden age" was coined by Hesiod, a Greek poet and rhapsode who lived around 800 B.C. Even he thought the age he lived in sucked. It is 2800 years down the road, so our present age must be sucking even harder.

Not everyone agrees with me. In fact, no one agrees with me. Everyone looks back, as if there were a period in history when, if history had only stopped there, everything would have been fine.

Really? When was a better time? When was a better time than right this minute?

I couldn't care less if people are self-deluded in their fantasies about the past. Only now those very self-deluded people are the exact people in power. And their nostalgia has a sinister tinge. Cuz they don't want to go back to a time that was. They want to go back to a time that wasn't. Their idea of the "good old days" was cranked out by frightened TV sitcom writers, shortsighted pundits, and cynical Hollywood producers.

Move aside and shut up. And stop making hell on earth for those of us who are moving forward.

WHAT AN EXCELLENT DAY FOR AN EXORCISM

In the 1973 blockbuster film *The Exorcist*, the evil spirit possessing twelve-year-old Linda Blair and causing her to levitate, self-mutilate, masturbate, rotate, and vomit with fire-hose force is not the devil himself but a demon named Pazuzu (a fact made a bit more clear in the William Peter Blatty novel on which the film was based).

The ancient Babylonians believed in a she-demon named Lamastu, who was a constant threat to infants and pregnant women; she is a distant foremother of the similarly baby-stealing Lilith. Pazuzu (also "Pizuzu"), a bit of a wild-card wind demon, was generally malevolent, but as a rival of Lamastu's, he would often force the she-demon back to the underworld rather than let her attack an infant. So, oddly enough, amulets of evil Pazuzu were sometimes hung in the homes of newborns or worn by pregnant women.

In surviving Babylonian statuary, we can see that Pazuzu was a rather peculiar assemblage of parts. He had one or more pairs of wings, a dog's head, huge taloned feet, and—Hey ladies!—a snake-headed penis.

In the *Exorcist* book and film, Pazuzu is unleashed during an archaeological dig near the once great Assyrian city of Nineveh. Early on, the demon himself gets a few moments of unpossessive screen time in the form of a statuette, and later during the climactic exorcism scene as a looming, malevolent presence.

DAEVA STYLE

Demons became very active players in the cosmology of Zoroastrianism, and a precise demonology was described in the Avesta, the holy text of the Mazdean sect of the religion. Good god Ahura Mazda has an army of holy spirits (the ahura) to assist him, but they are nearly equally matched by evil god Ahriman and his legion of demons, or daevas.

The daevas had a strict hierarchical structure according to their powers and responsibilities, with the top seven archdemons individually overseeing the spread of faithlessness, chaos, wickedness, disobedience, hunger, thirst, and lies. Often the archdemons are somewhat faceless and workmanlike, but even so a few personalities emerge: Aka Manah spreads his wickedness primarily by inducing unnatural desires. Chaos-demon Aesma is a bristling, irrational bundle of explosive rage, vengeful wrath, and violent fury—the demon most likely to be ejected from an anger management session. There was also Druj or Drug ("droog"), a female demon who embodied all womanly forms of evil wrapped up in one sweet corrupted package ("Drugs" was later used to describe a general variety of demons).

One portion of the Avesta, the Vendidad, describes situations where philosopher/prophet Zoroaster (aka Zarathustra) has his holiness and dedication questioned, challenged, and seriously tested by daevas—beginning with the assassin demon Buiti, whose sneaky "invisible death" powers are only undone when Zarathustra loudly recites his prayers. This general setup—holy man besieged by cunning evil spirits—is echoed frequently in the trial-by-demons of early Christian saints.

I'VE FALLEN AND I CAN'T GET UP

One of the most common points of origin for devils and demons is rather unlikely: They hail not from hell but from heaven. The presence of evil in a cosmos created by a benevolent God is the result of devils and demons who were once angels and who fell—or were pushed—out of heaven because of acts of arrogance and rebellion. Demon pride never ends well.

In the Hebrew Bible, Isaiah 14 speaks of the fall of Lucifer, though Lucifer here, meaning "bright star," may refer to a corrupted earthly Babylonian king rather than to Satan. But the dynamic of the account is what matters: A "star" who wishes to be godlike, or even superior to God, becomes a victim of his own arrogance and narcissism and crashes down from the heights of heaven to the depths of the underworld. In Judaic noncanonical works such as *The Book of Watchers*, *The First Book of Enoch*, and *The Book of Jubilees*, this "fall" was expanded upon as a means of explaining the origin of Satan, along with his legion of demons. Early Christian writers expanded on this premise.

Though details shifted in various retellings, the basic account was that Lucifer, one of God's dearest and most trusted angels, was not happy in a subservient role to God and was jealous of the loving attention God lavished upon his creation of earth, man, and woman. Among the angels, Lucifer talked up plans for a power play and got a fair amount of support; in some versions one-third of the angels were willing to back him. Lucifer and company attempted to stage a sort of celestial coup d'état, but of course were defeated. They were, after all, up against the Supreme Being. Cast into hell for their wild insubordination, Lucifer transformed into Satan, and the fallen angels became demons.

An additional class of demons, the Nephilim, were said to be the offspring of fallen angels and human women. The basis for this belief was Genesis 6:1–4, in which the "sons of God saw the daughters of men that they were fair; and they took them wives of all which they chose." The idea of overheated bad-boy angels having their way with earth girls was something of a point of contention in the early church, as there was no scripture explicitly describing these "sons of God" as Satan's fallen angels. In the first book of Enoch, these fallen angels are known as "grigori" and are led by the demon Azazel. In addition to mating with a human wife, Azazel further spreads discord by teaching men how to make weapons with which to express their violence, and by teaching women how to apply cosmetics, the better to showcase their carnality.

BY NAME

Demons made it through translations into the Bible, though sometimes in shadowy form. It's not always clear whether certain named spirits of evil are a reference to Satan or to some other hellish entity. The ugly moniker "Belial" turns up in the Old and New Testament, seemingly as an alias of Satan. In the New Testament, Belial is contrasted as being as opposite to Christ as darkness is to light (2 Corinthians). But outside the Bible, Belial, whose name derived from a Hebrew phrase for worthlessness, was often depicted as a sergeant at arms for Satan, and a demon whose specialties included sloth, destructiveness, and impurity.

In Revelation 9:11, the king of hell has the Hebrew name of Abaddon, or the Greek name of Apollyon. These also became extrabiblical names for demons working under the command of Satan.

Likewise, the monstrous creatures Leviathan and Behemoth are described through some rather mystical language, particularly in the book of Job, as entities that may be menacing, but they are not explicitly from hell. In medieval illustrations, Leviathan might be depicted as a whale or a crocodile, but it might also be an apocalyptic she-dragon of the sea. Behemoth could be a hippopotamus, or perhaps a gigantic, ravenous, one-of-a-kind beast. Legend tended to cast these two as the world's largest demons, and in some Judaic writings the oversized pair are slain by God and turned into the hot entrées at a postapocalyptic banquet.

ANGELS ON WHEELS

The term "Hell's Angels" first became a pop-culture fixture after the release of Howard Hughes's 1930 film about a squadron of World War I Royal Air Force aces (the first multimillion-dollar feature ever made). During World War II, film fiction became military reality as a number of B-17 bombers and some entire fighter squadrons put the name "Hell's Angels" on their aircraft. The Flying Tigers Pursuit Squadron of P-40 aircraft, with the famous "Tiger Shark" smile around the front of the planes, were also referred to as Hell's Angels.

Connections between the Nazi-battling pilots and the more familiar, motorist-startling bikers are tenuous. Stories that the bikers were originally a group of rowdy, hard-drinking ex-pilots who wanted to keep the wartime thrills a-coming seem spurious. Nonetheless, in 1948, in Fontana, California, a first group of renegade motorcycle enthusiasts dropped an apostrophe and officially formed the first chapter of the Hells Angels Motorcycle Club (Hells Angels, in any spelling, is now a fiercely protected copyright of the club).

DJINN SIN

While Christianity's Satan commands his legion of demons, in Islamic beliefs, Shaytan has an army of evil spirits, alternately known as djinn, jinn, or genies. The djinn work with their evil leader to tempt souls, but they are of a more ambiguous nature than Christian demons, and some of them are capable of benevolent actions. Djinn were originally created from a fiery substance and were believed to be able to assume human or animal form in order to exert their influence over humans. But they are also capable of bestowing supernatural abilities upon those who summon them. This element of their makeup has been played upon both in Arabic folklore (*1001 Arabian Nights*) and in the Western imagination's vision of lamp-locked genies. (The tales of Aladdin and his genie don't seem to be of purely Arabic origin, and are thought to be a Westernized addition to the *Arabian Nights* stories.)

The djinn offer an interesting example of what can happen when an evil spirit crosses cultures: What starts out as a frightening demon can end up as a sitcom plot device or a family-friendly cartoon character.

Quite a few demons turn up for some significant crossing of paths with men of the New Testament. In Acts 16, the Apostle Paul performs an exorcism, driving a demon out of a slave girl. Unfortunately, the demon had been supplying the slave with fortune-telling powers, which made money for her masters. Once the spirit is driven out, and the girl loses her powers of divination, the masters are enraged and promptly beat and imprison Paul.

More significantly, Jesus—God living as man—does quite a bit of direct battle with demons, frequently casting them out of afflicted humans. One of his most famous healings took place in the region of Gadara, or Gerasenes, east of the Jordan River, and is recounted in the Gospels of Matthew, Mark, and Luke. Jesus encounters a decrepit madman who has long been possessed by a multitude of demons. When Jesus asks his name, the man—or the spirits within—describe that multitude as "Legion." The demons beg Jesus not to send them back to the "deep" (presumably hell), and in a surprising act of mercy, Jesus agrees. Rather than being summarily banished to hell, the demons will be sent into the bodies of a nearby herd of pigs. The demons don't get quite the result they bargained for, however, for as soon as the pigs receive their demonic visitors, they rush over a steep cliff, plunge into the sea, and drown.

The man who has been exorcised has no recollection of his time as a demon-controlled entity, but the astounded locals fill him in on what Jesus has just done for him. He wants to join Jesus as an apostle, but Jesus instructs him to take on some missionary work instead and spread the word of his healing throughout his own city. The demon-free man gladly complies.

THE DETAILS ARE IN THE DEVILS

As the Christian idea of demons grew stronger at the end of the first millennium, there was an accompanying desire to organize and classify these agents of evil. One of the first comprehensive classifications was put together by Michael Constantine Psellus, an eleventh-century author, philosopher, and lecturer who lived and worked in both Athens and Constantinople. He wasn't strictly a theologian, and his writings covered politics, music, medicine, and language studies. But his demon classification was widely circulated, and it became the basis for many later similar classifications. For example, Francisco Guazzo, a sixteenth-century Milanese priest, used Psellus's work as the basis for his widely read who's who of the underworld, *Compendium Maleficarum*.

Psellus broke down the world of demons this way:

Air demons: They caused storms, thunder, and all bad weather.

Earth demons: The most treacherous, they hid all about a human's everyday life, and their mission was to tempt humans into sin.

Water demons: They created stormy seas, sunk ships, and drowned people.

Nether demons: They lived underground and were responsible for earthquakes, volcanoes, and crop failures.

Night demons: They could not stand the sunlight, but were adept at bringing horrid dreams and raging lusts while one sleeps.

Fire demons: Satan's private army, they would not be seen on earth until the Apocalypse.

HOT ENGINE

In 1971, looking to field an entry in the growing sporty coupe market, the Dodge division of

Chrysler packed a V8 engine into a restyled Plymouth body and gave it a name designed to grab some attention on the road: the Demon. In case any fellow drivers missed the name, the car came decorated with some hellish graphics: a tough little cartoon devil, complete with trident. Dodge didn't flinch from the Demon's underworld associations, and one souped-up model was called the Sizzler. The Demon was not particularly popular; in fact, it was markedly unpopular with some motorists—several religious groups let Dodge know that they were highly offended by the choice of name. Despite whatever help from the dark side the Demon might have expected, it was discontinued after the 1973 model year.

If not for some vagaries of the naming process, the Demon might have had some damned company during its brief life on the road. The Demon was patterned after the Plymouth Duster, which got its name from powerful, naturally occurring, dirt-throwing whirlwinds. Plymouth could have conceivably gone with another name used to describe such whirlwinds: Dust Devil.

WAR COUNCIL

In John Milton's *Paradise Lost* (1667), the great poet drew on a variety of historical sources and a number of familiar demons to populate one of the most striking visions of hell ever conceived. Once Lucifer and his fellow rebel angels are expelled from heaven shortly after the creation and hurled hellward, the devils quickly establish a pecking order and an assumption of individual responsibilities, the better to organize themselves into a demon army that can retake heaven, or at least rule hell.

Lucifer becomes Satan, hell's leader. Having decided to make a home on the side of a netherworld volcano, Satan utilizes the talents of Mulciber (a demon based upon Vulcan, the Roman god of fire and volcanoes) in order to serve as a draftsman and Mammon to serve as contractor to build a splendid hell palace, called Pandaemonium ("All demons").

As far as the chain of command goes, Satan's second-in-command is Beelzebub, the demon of envy. The highest-ranking councillors are the ever-angry, quick-to-war Moloch; the slothful, "why-bother-with-war" Belial; and—doing double-duty—Mammon, a demon of avarice who seems to think the fires of hell aren't so bad once you get used to them (he feels that the abundant gems and gold of hell can make the getting used to easy).

In Book II of the twelve-book epic, each demon gets a chance to make his case for what he sees as the most prudent course of action. Moloch wants to continue a bloody, head-to-head battle with God and the angels. Belial and Mammon want to give up and make the best of the hell around them. Beelzebub slyly comes up with a third tactic; instead of attacking heaven, the devils can go after God's cherished creations—earth, the Garden of Eden, and Adam and Eve. There is an open and free-wheeling demonic debate about who's got the best idea, but ultimately head honcho Satan sides with Beelzebub.

After a rather difficult and confusing journey to the earth, Satan turns up in the Garden of Eden, sets his sights on Eve, and manages to instigate the Fall of Man, introducing into the world Sin and Death. (The pair are presented as Satan's plucky, resourceful, thoroughly evil daughter and son: The daughter, Sin, sprang whole from Satan's head. The son, Death, is the result of Satan/Sin incest). Satan returns to Pandaemonium, expecting to pitch a hell of a victory party, but when he announces his triumph, all he hears is hissing. God has turned all his fellow devils into miserable snakes. A grove of trees that pops up in hell seems to offer at least the consolation prize of some tasty fruit, but in a fittingly poetic twist God has designed the fruit to turn to ashes in the snakes' mouths whenever they take a bite.

Satan has no choice but to sulk and bide his time, until he gets another crack at humanity in Milton's epic sequel, *Paradise Regained*.

HELL NOISE

Paradise Lost is not only the name of one of the most significant works of literature in the English language, it's also the name of a long-running British progressive metal band. The band proudly likens their sound to the sounds Milton described beyond hell's gates: "torment, and loud lament, and furious rage." Their releases include *Gothic*, *Shades of God*, *Believe in Nothing*, and the slightly more optimistic *Symbol of Life*.

SINFUL SEVEN

One of the most aggressive, ruthless, and lethal witch-hunters of the sixteenth century was Peter Binsfeld, a Jesuit bishop of Trier, Germany. His *Treatise on Confessions by Evildoers and Witches* (1589) was considered a highly useful, legally solid, witch-finder's manual. (In it, he revealed one of his key witch-finding philosophies: that nonlethal torture did not really constitute torture at all.) Binsfeld was almost certainly the prosecuting force behind the deaths of countless men, women, and children.

Binsfeld suggested that certain key devils and demons were aligned with each of the seven deadly sins. In his formation:

- Lucifer = pride
- Mammon = greed
- Asmodeus = lust
- Beelzebub = gluttony
- Leviathan = envy
- Belphegor = sloth
- Satan = anger

ROGUES' GALLEY

A few random, demonically bad apples:

- **BELPHEGOR:** A demon whose specialty is to suck humans into get-rich-quick schemes,

Belphegor appeals to humanity's inherent laziness. He's at his peak powers in April (a tax-season coincidence?) and, depending on the demonologist, can appear either as a beautiful woman or an unsightly, naked old man. French occultist Collin de Plancy claimed that Belphegor was hell's special envoy to Paris.

- **CARNIVEAN:** Early Christian writers described Carnivean as the patron devil of lewd and obscene behavior. Wherever people were acting shamelessly, Carnivean was assumed to be at work. He was said to be invoked by witches during sabbats, and he never, ever missed an orgy.

- **MASTEMA:** Mastema gets his name from the Hebrew word for hostility or hatred. In *The Book of Jubilees*, Mastema pleads with God after Noah survives the flood to let a few demons survive as well, and God consents. In *Jubilees*, Mastema is also the spirit that kills off Egypt's firstborn during the tenth plague.

- **ROSIER:** Not all demons have gone for over-the-top displays of sex and violence. Medieval Christian mythology gave rise to Rosier, a fallen angel who became the patron devil of seduction. Rather than simply serving as a catalyst for fornication, Rosier worked like an evil Cupid, deriving great pleasure from causing people to fall in love and then act like idiots.

- **SAMMAEL:** A demon who harks back to Talmudic lore, Sammael can present himself as a fierce destroyer or a supersmooth seducer. Sometimes his name seems to serve as an alias for Satan; more often he is a separate figure who serves as an angel of death.

WITCHES VERSUS DEMONS

Sounds like it might make for a pretty good cage match. In northern Italy during the sixteenth century, there was a pitched battle between witches and demons that was resolved, in the demons' favor, only with help from the witch-hunters of the ongoing Inquisition.

The witches in this case were not quite witches in the satanic sense, but *benandanti*—"good walkers"—a loosely organized corps of shamans and shamanesses who used white magic—benevolent spells and incantations—to protect crops and livestock from the meddling of *malandanti*, or evil demons. It was believed that benandanti, who could be identified at birth by the membranous cauls on their heads, left their bodies at night in spirit form to fight off the assaults of evil spirits that might otherwise bring death and disease to a village. In *Night Battles* by historian Carlo Ginzburg, a highly significant exploration of the medieval witch hunts, the benandanti are described as respected and welcomed members of the community in the eyes of the peasants whose farms they protected. Benandanti were particularly active in the Friuli region of the scattered Lombard dukedom, where they were seen not as spooky sorcerers, but as practitioners of rites that fit in with ancient folk tradition. In their willingness to use their spirit abilities to take on evil demons, they were considered to be doing holy work, and were not seen as a threat to local clergy or authorities.

That started to change when agents of the Inquisition, under the direction of Vatican-appointed chief witch-hunters Heinrich Kramer and Jacob Sprenger, began turning up in Friuli. At first, Inquisitors may have been a bit confused about how to proceed. Their mandate was to seek out agents of Satan, and finding "good witches" who were working with the blessing of the local church was a puzzler. But a letter from Pope

Alexander VI in 1501 to Angelo of Verona, the Inquisitor of Lombardy, clarified the situation: There were no such thing as good witches. Accordingly, the benandanti were at least heretics and at worst in league with the devil; and all Inquisitors should ignore the protestations of local churches and secure and punish all witches, as the Pope put it, "through the medium of justice." The Inquisition's idea of the medium of justice was, of course, extensive, horrendous torture, and it wasn't long before flayed and scourged benandanti were admitting to being witches of the Satan-loving, evildoing variety.

With the benandanti out of the way thanks to the Inquisition, the evil demons were up against no resistance. They seem to have made the most of it. By the mid-1800s, Friuli and the surrounding regions were devastated by famine.

MY HELL

MOLLY HASKELL
Author, film critic

If hell exists, I'd imagine it as the Luis Bunuel film *The Exterminating Angel*; or worse: you're stuck throughout infinity with all the people you've avoided on earth.

I think the notion of hell serves a purpose, at the very minimum as a still pungent expletive. Why? Because we're not quite sure there isn't an afterlife and some form of retribution. So even if it's internalized or metaphorical, hell means the Very Worst, whatever that might be (and all the more ominous because undefined) and something utterly out of our control. At the same time, it's slightly reassuring, giving meaning to death, which is otherwise devoid of meaning.

GRIM WORK

From the twelfth to the eighteenth century, Christian demonology became an increasingly hot area of study. While it was up to clergy and church leaders to properly interpret the Bible as a holy text, a number of scientists, philosophers, and theologians took it upon themselves to sketch out precise hierarchies of the underworld, including names, ranks, and descriptions of all the demons one might find there. These writings often took the form of "grimoires"—from the same root as "grammar"—a kind of beginner's guide to the world of demons that was complete with incantations, instructions for conjurations, and special prayers. Most grimoires were not to be confused with darker, openly satanic works that celebrated the demon world. Grimoires were manuals to the workings of hell that, while drawing on ancient traditions of mysticism and magic, were very clear about their sense of Christian piety. If human souls were to be well armed in their battles with hell's demons, the grimoire was a necessary report from behind enemy lines.

One of the most widely distributed grimoires was *The Lesser Key of Solomon* (in Latin, *Lemegeton Clavicula Salomonis*). The collection of text took its name from King Solomon of the Bible.

Solomon was a son of David and Bathsheba, who became a king of Israel and a builder of Jerusalem's great temple. During his forty-year reign he was a powerful, unifying force for his kingdom, to which he brought a good deal of wealth. For most of the time he served as king, he was considered to be an exceptionally wise ruler, but toward the end of his reign he became a decadent figure (if having seven hundred wives and three hundred concubines qualifies one as decadent). Solomon turned

249

away from God to worship many of the hometown idols of his far-flung female companions. That last stretch of his story inspired medieval writers, who imagined that in Solomon's dabbling with various pagan religions he had become a kind of master occultist. In fact, one potent bit of jewelry that turns up in Jewish, Islamic, and Christian legend is the Seal of Solomon, a signet ring marked with varying religious symbols that was said to have the power to conjure and command demonic forces.

Parts of the *Lesser Key of Solomon* date to the thirteenth century, and it seems to have been assembled into a somewhat standard form by the end of the sixteenth century. *The Lesser Key of Solomon* is separated into four distinct sections:

- the Goetia, the primary work of demonology, that describes itself as a comprehensive presentation of all the spirits that Solomon ever spoke with ("hadd any converse with");
- the Theurgia Goetia, which lists spirits of the air, who may be of good or evil nature;
- the Ars Paulina, which sets out an intricate system of astrology;
- the Ars Almadel Salomonis, which lists the twenty spirits that govern the zodiac

Later editions of the work contain a fifth section, the Ars Notoria, which contains orations and prayers supposedly spoken by Solomon in his temple.

For demon purposes, the place to look is the Goetia. Here, the seventy-two chief spirits an adept magician might conjure are described, with each being given a rank of king, duke, prince, marquis, president, earl, or knight. The metallurgy of each spirit's secret ring is described, along with its planetary alignment, and in some illustrated editions the demonic seals and symbols are drawn. The purpose of the Goetia is to summon these often difficult-to-control beings in order to get them to do your bidding. Not all spirits are exclusively evil, but many have some strange powers that can certainly get mortals into trouble.

The top spirit king in this hierarchy is a fellow named Bael, who has the power to make men disappear and who can take the form of a cat, a toad, or a man. It is also noted that (like a demonic Don Corleone) "he speaketh very horsly."

A few other standout spirits:

- **Sitri:** A prince who appears as a winged leopard. He has the power to inflame men with lust for women, inflame women with lust for men, and to "causeth them to shew themselves naked."
- **Leraye:** A marquis who appears as an archer. He instigates

battles and violent contests, and causes the wounds that might result from such fights to putrefy.

- **Glasya Labolas:** A president who takes the form of a winged dog. He can be summoned either for his fortune-telling abilities or his ability to incite manslaughter.
- **Furcas:** A knight who turns up as a cranky old man on a horse. As an expert in philosophy, rhetoric, and logic, he can cloud any issue you might like clouded.
- **Belial:** He's here, in the form of a beautiful angel riding a chariot of fire. He will appear boasting (in a deep, beautiful voice) of his close association with Lucifer, but if properly placated with gifts and sacrifices, he will become a master of dirty politics for you, a nefarious campaign manager for your social or professional life.

BUS PASSES

Demons have long been associated with sexual misbehavior, and in medieval legendry two forms of particularly lusty demons focused on nothing but sexual hijinks. These were the incubus and the succubus (plural being incubi and succubi). The names themselves made clear their sexual disposition: "incubus" derives from the Latin for "to lie upon," this being the male demon; "succubus" derives from the Latin for "to lie under," this being the female. Incubi and succubi would visit a victim at night and have sex with them while they slept. Any nocturnal arousals or overtly carnal dreams could be blamed on a visit from one of these spirits. Men experiencing daytime exhaustion might also suspect that they had been the victim of demonic lovemaking. According to the witch-hunters' guide, *Malleus Maleficarum*, succubi would sometimes steal the semen of the men they copulated with and turn the substance over to incubi, who would then proceed to impregnate unsuspecting women with demon spawn (and what parent hasn't suspected, in the darkest of moments, that there was demon spawn in the house?).

For those who thought they might not mind these sorts of demonic encounters—the more pleasurable the episode with a demon lover, the closer one had stepped to damnation.

LIKE A VIRGIN

The book of Tobit (Tobias) is deuterocanonical scripture: It's part of the Greek translations of the Hebrew

Bible (the Septuagint) and is found in the Roman Catholic Bible and the Eastern Orthodox Bible, but it was considered to be apocrypha by Protestant Reformers.

Tobit's story contains a rather unusual demon episode: A woman named Sarah—a virgin—marries a man, but on their wedding night, before the marriage can be consummated, the demon Asmodeus kills the groom. This happens six more times: Sarah marries, takes her man to the marriage bed, and finds her new husband slain by Asmodeus before she has the chance to become a nonvirgin (apparently the word on Sarah didn't spread too quickly among local eligible bachelors). Tobit marries Sarah, and the angel Raphael steps in to banish Asmodeus, allowing husband and wife to successfully conjugate. It turns out that the previous seven husbands had approached their wedding night with lust, rather than a sense of sanctity, so God allowed Asmodeus to do away with them. Tobit is more pious and God-fearing, so he is allowed to proceed.

The story is strange in that the demon seems to be committing manslaughter as an enforcer of piety rather than as an agent of evil. It also seems unduly harsh that those first seven husbands would not be allowed at least a bit of lust on their honeymoon.

CHECKERED PAST

While demonologists of the past seem to have prided themselves on taking a completist approach to their work, they couldn't quite foresee demons to come. Brand-new, uncharted lesser devils have continued to pop up on the pop-culture hellscape.

One of the more recent hellions would be the Checkered Demon, a creation of legendary underground comics illustrator S. Clay Wilson, and frequent star of the boundary-smashing series of Zap Comix. Zap, which was published from 1967 to 1998, was the lovingly twisted brainchild of artists Robert Crumb, Rick Griffin, Gilbert Shelton, and Victor Moscoso, along with Wilson. It celebrated in bold, inky fashion everything that the censorious Comics Code Authority of the 1950s and 1960s had sought to prevent from appearing in comic books: rampant drug use, sexual perversion, and outright degeneracy.

Even among the stiff competition of fellow Zap characters, the Checkered Demon emerged as a heroic figure of bad behavior, a foul-mouthed, beer-swilling malcontent who rarely encounters an orifice that he does not come to know intimately. The demon was aptly named: He's a squat, ugly fellow with standard horns and tail, whose only article of clothing—his snazzy checkered slacks—help to conceal his enormous and often quite active genitals.

The Checkered Demon differs from his demonic brethren throughout history in that he is not particularly interested in instigating or inducing sinfulness among mortals. In fact, he would often much prefer to keep to himself, but finds himself drawn into various, messy misadventures when he ventures out into a sin-ridden aboveground world. In one epic tale, the demon seeks nothing more than a peaceful nap, but is continually disturbed by the rowdy comings and goings of local biker gangs, among other distractions. The understandably cranky demon thus finds it necessary to murder, swindle, pummel, and fornicate his way toward finding a quiet, restful place to catch some shuteye (He eventually finds that place—on a cot in Home Sweet Hell).

Oddly enough, the name "Checkered Demon" also carries with it a frighteningly wholesome, outdoorsy connotation. It's the nickname of a mountain in California's High Sierras that has become exceptionally popular with ice climbers.

DEMONS WITH SHOVELS

In European demonology, spirits were sometimes of ambiguous nature, capable of good or evil. In some Scandinavian demonologies, demons were in fact more akin to helpful elves, and they turned nasty only when humans got in the way of their work.

Swedish clergyman Olaus Magnus was one of the most accomplished geographers of the sixteenth century, but in his massive treatise *A Description of the Northern Peoples*, he included folk accounts of Scandinavian demons. According to some of these legends, certain demons of the North were not particularly concerned with assaulting humans—they were sometimes more happy to work in stables at night, cleaning them out and feeding the animals. In fact, it was believed that the animals sometimes preferred their demon attendants to their human stablemen.

PRAY UPON

One of the earliest postbiblical Christians to do some notable battling with demons was Saint Anthony, a fourth-century ascetic often cited as the first monk. He was the child of a well-to-do family in Egypt, but one day while attending a Christian church service, he heard a piece of scripture—words of Christ—that resonated deeply with him: "If thou wilt be perfect, go and sell that thou hast, and give to the poor, and thou shalt have treasure in heaven; and come and follow me" (Matthew 19:21). He took those words to heart almost immediately, giving up all his possessions, moving into a tomb at the outskirts of his city, and starting a life as a secluded, solitary hermit.

While Anthony was there, the devil went after him by sending a series of tormenting demons. Sometimes these spirits were in the form of tempting women, but more frequently they were in the form of wild animals—wolves, lions, snakes, scorpions, and demonic beasts. Saint Anthony got roughed up considerably, but he came to realize that his prayers were stronger than the demons. By invoking the name of

God, he could make the snarling demons disappear in puffs of smoke.

Saint Anthony's battles with demons were an inspiration for a wide range of artists, including Bosch, Cézanne, Dürer, Orsi, Schongauer, and Grünewald.

EVERYTHING YOU SAY IS A LIE

With various demonologies circulating through seventeenth-century Europe and the very concept of demonology gaining a widespread popularity, both Catholic and Protestant churches found it necessary to take an official stand on such non-church-sanctioned works. One frequently held position was that demonologies could not be trusted because of their very nature: Since the source of the information they contained originated from Satan, the Great Obfuscator and Father of All Lies, it was to be expected that the works would be riddled with errors and falsehoods that, rather than protecting a demon conjurer (or reader), would in fact put him in league with the devil.

SOUNDS LIKE . . .

Esteemed modern composer Michael Colgrass wrote his 1983 piece *Demon* for amplified piano, orchestra, alto sax, tape machine, and three radios.

BLAME IT ON DEMONS?

Johann Weyer (sometimes referred to as Wier or Wierus) was a Dutch-born physician and demonologist who advanced the understanding of demons with a pair of major late-sixteenth-century works, *De Praestigiis Daemonum* and *Pseudomonarchia Daemonum*. In the latter, Weyer presents a list of conjurable spirits that closely follows the Goetia, although often with more descriptive detail. For instance, the conjurations for "Beliall" include a minihistory on how this particular devil was once locked up in a brass urn at the bottom of a sea, but was inadvertently freed by treasure-hunting Babylonians.

There's a bit of a twist to Weyer's demonology. While he seems to accept without question the existence of demons, he was horrified by the excesses of the European witch hunts and thought that no godly work was being done through them. So, while portions of his work read like a straightforward demonology, his is also given to anti-Catholic diatribes as well as some groundbreaking theories at what might be at the root cause of witchy behavior: mental illness. In fact, he is sometimes considered "the father of modern psychiatry" for being among the first to recognize that such an illness of the mind was possible.

While the title of his latter work, literally the *Pseudo-monarchy of Demons*, seems to indicate that he might undo some demon beliefs from earlier times, his demon hierarchy is just as extensive, and his Satan is perhaps even more powerful a figure than the one allegedly worshipped by presumed witches. His ability to see through the brutality and false accusations of the witch hunts, and at the same time scientifically catalog demons, makes him a strange and contradictory figure in hell history.

YES, BLAME THE DEMONS

Some in his own time found Johann Weyer not only strange, but indictable.

Jean Bodin, a French jurist and the author of extensive

works on the nature of politics and nationhood, might well be considered a leading political theorist of the sixteenth century. But while Bodin's political works are notable for their humane approach to the art of governance, and for their emphasis on tolerance and accommodation in an era when bloody territorial wars were the norm, the humane side of Bodin apparently did not extend to those accused of witchcraft. His 1580 handbook for judges presiding over witchcraft trials, *Démonomanie des Sorciers*, not only promoted the idea that humans were under widespread threat from demons and witches, but it also specifically beat up on Weyer's theories. Bodin found it despicable that a learned man could ignore the empirical evidence of witchcraft all around him and come up with the ridiculous notion of mental illness. To Bodin, there was only one logical explanation: Weyer must be a witch himself.

FOREWARNED

In February 2005, the big-budget, special effects–laden feature film *Constantine*, starring Keanu Reeves (and based on the Hellblazer comics), was assigned an R rating because it contained violence and demonic images.

Weyer managed to escape prosecution (Bodin had explicitly called for it), and eventually some of his ideas began to take hold. Some of Weyer's theories were expounded upon in the work of Reginald Scot, a sixteenth-century author (whose day job was serving as justice of the peace in Kent, England.) In his 1584 work, *Discoverie of Witchcraft*, he includes Weyer's list of conjurable demons, but surrounds them with much more pointed observations about demonology, witchcraft, alchemy, astrology, and fortune-telling, all of which he essentially pronounces to be so much bunk.

Like Weyer, Scot includes some wild, anti-Catholic diatribes, going so far as to assert that witches and demons, or at least the illusion of witches and demons, are the invention of self-aggrandizing priests. Scot is also clearly disturbed at what he sees to be the driving force behind the witch hunts: the desire of male authority figures to ravish, torment, and otherwise take advantage of vulnerable women.

Scot doesn't just catalog demons; he also exposes all the methods by which one human can appear to possess demonic powers. In other words, he gives away a lot of magic tricks. The secrets to a great number of feats of legerdemain and mentalism are explained, and Scot includes almost step-by-step instructions to such "stage magic" illusions as how to make a severed head come to life and how to make a recently hanged man appear to come back to life. He is a fan of such magic, as long as it is presented as entertainment rather than as the work of the devil.

And while he concedes the devil is a real threat to humanity's well-being, the demons, in general, are a useless illusion. In one especially sharp chapter toward the end of his work, (Chapter XXXIX, to be precise), Scot contends that all those who have claimed to see or hear spirits, demons, angels, and evidence of witchcraft are actually suffering from such simple human frailties as depression, fear, self-delusion, mental illness, poor eyesight, or drunkenness.

Scot's final point is this: The only truth a believer needs is that of Jesus Christ. The demons and all the rest are a lot of nonsense. He predicts that this point of view will spread with the rather neat closing couplet, "What things soever snowe dooth hide, Heat of the sunne dooth make it spide."

ARMY DEMON

Another recent addition to modern demonology charts comes by way of the Hellboy comic books and graphic novels by Mike Mignola. Hellboy, who debuted in 1994, might be described as an occult detective who spends the bulk of his time fighting both crazed Nazi scientists and grotesque inhuman monsters. Hellboy was brought to the earth as a toddler toward the end of World War II after some imprecations from famously mad spiritualist Rasputin went awry. He was taken into custody by the U.S. Army and raised as a ward of the Bureau of Paranormal Research and Defense. Despite a somewhat cynical nature, Hellboy sides with humans and is generally a nice guy (although if genes turn out to be more important than environment, he may turn out to be the beast of the Apocalypse). In appearance, Hellboy is big and red and devilish, with a tail and a huge right hand made of stone, but in order to tone down his demonic side and appear a bit less intimidating, he keeps his horns sanded down to nubs.

In 2004, Hellboy made it to the big screen under the guidance of director Guillermo del Toro. The very human actor Ron Perlman was transformed into the demonic title character through the foam-latex ministrations of Academy Award–winning makeup artist Rick Baker.

FINAL POSSESSION

Among many other sports-minded nether-worlders: the Texas Panhandle's Dumas Demons, Pennsylvania's Kennett High School Blue Demons, Louisiana's Northwestern State Demons and Lady Demons, Duke University's Blue Devils, and New York's Freeport High School Red Devils.

Echoes of a very, very old rivalry? In January 2005 in Kansas, the Dodge City High School Red Demons varsity basketball team won its third consecutive Tournament of Champions title by defeating the Buhler Crusaders.

In Oklahoma, in the small town of Dibble, the high school varsity teams, the Demons, have repeatedly withstood religious protests over the name. As *Fort Worth Star-Telegram* columnist Bud Kennedy asked in a 2003 article, "If Satan wanted to *promote* devil worship, would he really name a team the Dibble Demons?"

ENDNOTE: DEMONS DUE

For all the trouble they've caused, it might be pointed out that demons have also allowed for a bit of cosmic humility on the part of troubled mortals. While a mortal might be reluctant to claim that the lord of darkness himself was taking time out of his evil master plans to fill an individual soul's day with a plague of minor misfortune, or to fill one with unseemly desires, or to turn one soul away from faith, such torments, travails, and spiritual corruption have always been the hellish bread and butter of the demons.

In almost every conception of hell, it has been demons who keep supply lines flowing by inducing wickedness among aboveground mortals, and it has been demons who have meted out specific punishments once a soul has been successfully secured for torment in the netherworld.

Demons are as old and universal as hell itself, and like their home turf, they are still flourishing as pivotal figures in religion, folklore, and popular imagination.

WHAT DO WE MAKE OF IT?

No one has ever written, painted, sculpted, modeled,
built, or invented except literally to get out of hell.
—Antonin Artaud

Let me go to hell, that's all I ask, and go on cursing them there,
and them look down and hear me, that might take some of
the shine off their bliss. —Samuel Beckett

For a place of pain and punishment, of fire and torment, hell has also demonstrated some surprising powers as a place of inspiration.

Our general understanding of what hell is and what it's there for has always come primarily from religious teachings. But for as long as the purpose and nature and existence of hell has been taught, writers, poets, artists, and thinkers have wanted to descend deeper—to expand, explain, and envision hell.

Some have used their creative talents to produce works that attempt to directly reflect religious doctrine. But many others have used the basics of hell as a starting point from which imagination might be unloosed. Michelangelo drew upon Revelation and a good deal of poetic license to paint the hellishly detailed depiction of the *Last Judgment* for the Sistine Chapel. Dante's *Inferno* was more a work of invention than scripture, but so powerful and well constructed was his hell that it has remained a hefty piece of cultural netherworld bedrock. There's faith and piety in the work of Hieronymus Bosch, but his proto-surreal, phantasmagoric paintings of hell presented a view of the place unlike any that had come before—a vista of fresh nightmares that still have the power to shock and terrify.

And entertain. That's the odd thing about hell as inspiration: The place has not just produced artwork intended to instruct, warn, and frighten. Hell art, like any art, has always sought to engage an audience, and fear is only one way to get that audience to pay attention. Yes, Bosch's hell is scary, but it's also packed with comedy, a comedy that comes from our recognition of all that is silly, hypocritical, and generally flawed in our character (well, not *our* character—those other wicked people's character).

As a creative source, hell has been tapped as inspiration for every possible genre of tale, from love story to adventure yarn to serious drama to pitch-black satire to lowest of lowbrow comedy. Right from the time of the very first underworlds, society-at-large has been able to embrace a soul-deep contradiction between hell as mortifying realm of eternal damnation and hell as compelling subject for earthly entertainment. And as an audience, if the last few millennia are any indication, our curiosity and fascination with the place haven't flagged a bit.

Just what exactly do we make of hell?

Here's what a few notable talents have done with it:

GOING DUTCH

While Dante laid out the literary blueprint for hell, the actual visuals for the place were conjured most power-fully and disturbingly by Hieronymus Bosch, a fifteenth-century Flemish painter. In Bosch's works, all the gory, gruesome, nightmarish horrors of hell that might previ-ously have been left to the medieval imagination were spread out boldly and explicitly for all mortals to wit-ness. All the fire, torture, mutilation, and degradation were there, along with many highly innovative depictions of what punishments might be meted out (among more traditional maimings and mutilations, sinners might be consumed by demonic rodents, violated with a woodwind instrument, dipped into slime, or kissed by a pig).

It's clear from his work that Bosch was both fascinated and darkly inspired by the idea of human sin—enough to make it a career-long specialty. Why? Hard to say, as little is actually known about Bosch's background. He was born Jerome van Aken in what would now be part of the Netherlands somewhere around the mid-1400s, and took his nom-de-paint from the town he grew up in, Hertogenbosch. He came from a family of painters, from whom he ostensibly learned his craft. He married somewhere around 1480, and seems to have lived a quiet, small-town life until his death in 1516.

But no matter his presumed lack of worldly experience and hands-on sinning, Bosch took hold of traditions, legends, folklore, and visions of hell that stretched from the moralistic to the parodic to the pornographic, and blended it all into his own strange and sharp-eyed view of what went on there. He also packed his paintings with symbolism and satire that would register with the audience of his day. He lived at a time when there was great upheaval in the church and tension between conservative and reform points of view, but Bosch doesn't seem to have shied from making clear in his paintings his personal feelings on political and religious issues of the day. On the contrary, some very surprised-looking priests and nuns are frequently savaged among the members of the wicked.

One of the conventional forms for painters of Bosch's time was the triptych, a huge work spread across three separate wooden panels and often used as an altarpiece. Bosch created a number of these, as well as individual works, and his reputation and popularity spread enough that some of his hellish paintings were done for foreign commissions. Others traveled afar into the hands of collectors (King Philip II of Spain, who oversaw much of the horrendous carnage of the Spanish Inquisition, seems to have been an avid fan). The sin-oriented nature of Bosch's work is clear in such works as *The Temptation of Saint Anthony* (featuring plenty of demons as well as a Satanic Black Mass), *The Conjurer*, *The Mocking of Christ*, *Ship of Fools*, and the straightforwardly titled *Paradise and Hell*.

Bosch's visions are both brilliant and terrifying, mixing an accomplished naturalist approach with freaky, bad-dream imagery that prefigures surrealism (Hello, Dali). Most of his contemporaries were much more concerned with giving image to the uplifting idea of salvation, but for Bosch, damnation was clearly a more inspiring muse. Here's a descriptive glimpse into a few of his hell visions:

The Seven Deadly Sins: You are being watched. The centerpiece of this work is a gigantic eye—the eye of God (with Christ inside the pupil)—which is clearly taking notice of all the highly stylized sinful transgressions happening around it. To drive the point home, images of a deathbed scene, the Last Judgment, heaven, and hell fill out the four corners of the work.

The Haywain: Lay off the fiber. This triptych shows the path of human wickedness, from the Fall in the Garden of Eden, to unchecked sinfulness on earth, to a final destination of hell. The interesting twist is that in the earthly central panel, sin is represented as an overflowing wagonload of hay, which those members of a crowd not otherwise distracted by corrupt behavior (drinking, fighting, murdering) are ready to pounce upon, much to the wagon-toting demons' delight. In the fiery vision of hell, sinners are either used as cheap labor or attacked and consumed by a weird assortment of demons that seem put together with animal parts and hellacious machinery. (Bosch's vision of Eden isn't such a paradise either—one can see Lucifer's fallen angels tumbling from heaven, transformed into grotesque insect demons.)

The Garden of Earthly Delights: Perhaps Bosch's most famous and recognizable work, it's also a thoroughly original and highly unconventional depiction of hell. This is a triptych, with the center panel showing those sinful earthly delights of the title, the left panel showing the Garden of Eden, and the right panel showing hell. Outer shutters to the work depict the world's creation. The way it scans, one moves from the somewhat surreal paradise of the garden, to an earth in which scores of nude men and women cavort in an orgiastic tableau of happy, and somewhat innocent-looking, sinfulness.

In the hell panel, the happiness and innocence are gone, and it's the demons' turn to cavort. Against a vista of smoky, fiery devastation, sinners are gnawed, nibbled, humiliated, impaled, and forced to entertain their demonic hosts. Many of the implements of torture are musical instruments, and the fellow strung up on the harp looks to be in particular agony.

The Last Judgment: In this triptych, Bosch skips the fleeting pleasures of earthly sins entirely and reduces the three-part story to paradise, where the Fall of Man is in motion; the Last Judgment, in which the wicked are pursued by a nightmarish demon army; and hell, where the sinners are fittingly probed, impaled, boiled, and burned.

GOIN' DOWN TO . . .

Hell frequently turns up in animated form as a setting on *South Park*, the blackly satirical and exuberantly foul-mouthed cartoon created by Matt Stone and Trey Parker. The depravity on display in *South Park*'s hell is firmly within the centuries-old tradition of hell-based entertainments that depicted vulgarity and immorality with unchecked gusto (farting demons were a familiar laugh producer in Middle Ages mystery plays). But even by the medieval standards of potty-humored mystery plays and near-pornographic apocalyptic tracts, Stone and Parker have fired things up a notch.

In the *South Park* cosmos, it turns out that the only true religion is Mormonism (although in one episode God admits to being a Buddhist). Mormons go to heaven; everyone else goes to hell. Hell is ruled by Satan, who lives in the River Styx Condominiums. Despite his fearsome, red, horned, barrel-chested appearance, he is a big softie, a sensitive, misunderstood loner who also happens to be gay. His on-again, off-again lover is Saddam Hussein, who arrived in hell after being mauled by wild boars. Hussein is an abusive sex addict, while Satan would like to spend more time cuddling.

The show has been successful enough that its "Satan" is currently available as both a plush toy and a posable action figure.

A HELL IN THE FAMILY

The renown of Bosch's work had both an artistic influence and a commercial impact on the sixteenth-century northern European art scene. A number of painters realized that not only were disturbing hellscapes not taboo, but such paintings were precisely what a certain segment of the well-to-do was willing to spend big bucks on.

Among the artists that succeeded Bosch was a notable family of painters: the Brueghels, which included father Pieter and sons Pieter and Jan. Father Brueghel—eventually known as Pieter the Elder—was not particularly hell-bent. He picked up the nickname "Peasant" Brueghel for his depictions of country life, pastoral landscapes, and gently satirical depictions of villagers indulging in the seven deadly sins. He did have a darker streak, evident in work such as *The Tower of Babel*, *The Fall of the Rebel Angels*, and in one of his most memorable works, *The Triumph of Death*, in which a terrifying army of skeletons vanquishes helpless souls (the point being not so much that those souls are hellbound, but that no soul can escape death).

Younger son Jan picked up on his dad's lighter side. He specialized in bright, sunny landscapes and delicate still lifes of flowers and came to be known as "Velvet" Brueghel. But older brother Pieter (Pieter the Younger) went for the dark side. Many of his works (such as *The Harrowing of Hell*) were populated with deformed demons that rivaled the strangeness of Bosch's work, and he created so many vistas of fiery torment and random grotesquerie that he picked up a well-earned artistic nickname of his own: "Hell" Brueghel.

HELL IS FOR LOVERS

Artists and writers have often toyed with the idea that hell might actually be a more interesting place to reside than heaven. That idea gets a full airing in George Bernard Shaw's *Don Juan in Hell*, the third act of his 1902 play *Man and Superman* (*Don Juan* has frequently been staged as a stand-alone theater piece).

In various versions of the Don Juan legend, the don, a well-heeled bon vivant and expert seducer of women, is hauled off to hell by the ghost of a man Don Juan has killed—the father of a sweet young conquest. Shaw's version plays out as an extended dream sequence, wherein an extended discussion/debate on the meaning of love and life takes place between Don Juan, the father's ghost (in the form of a statue), the seduced girl (who went on to live a long life and is now very surprised to find herself down below), and the devil. Shaw's devil is a particularly interesting piece of work: a peevish, thin-skinned sentimentalist who according to stage directions is going prematurely bald.

As Don Juan explains hell to the new arrival (his one-time bedmate), conventional notions of heaven and hell are upended. For one thing, the wicked do not feel pain in hell; since the place is designed for them, they are quite comfortable. And many nonwicked individuals prefer to hang out there because, it is explained, "heaven is the most angelically dull place in all creation." Shaw's devil is quick to clarify that he was not thrown out of heaven, but that he left because he couldn't stand it. He set up hell to be a place where love and beauty, in all their sloppy, untamable grandeur, are celebrated. (All that love and beauty are beginning to irritate the heck out of a wearied Don Juan, and he will eventually head off to heaven because the statue assures him that there are no beautiful women there.)

The devil ends up making a rather forceful argument that the universe has no real purpose, but perhaps his best line stems from that peevishness of his: "The world cannot get along without me, but it never gives me credit for that."

MY HELL

ROSIE O'DONNELL

Comic, ex-talk-show host, blogger

What do I think the worst torment of hell would be? Becoming what you loathe.

BUILD IT YOURSELF

The LucasArts game Afterlife, released in 1996, offered players the unusual opportunity to design and manage their own heaven and hell for an alien planet. In this otherworldly version of sim games, players mapped out and constructed their afterlife realms, assigned souls to their final destinations in accordance with their vices and virtues, and made sure that appropriate rewards and punishments were handed out. Reincarnation stations also needed to be set up to accommodate those ready to cycle through another round of bodily existence. Demonic and angelic guides helped up to a point, but players needed to be ready to handle a heap of logistics. If things went well, the player scored Pennies from Heaven. But there was always the peril of the Heaven Nose (which sucked up bits of afterworld) or the insufferable Disco Inferno. And one couldn't slack off—if all the souls were not properly administrated, they ended up walking around cluelessly in Sim Limbo.

IT'S A SMALL WORLD AFTER HELL

One of the oddest and most hellish of the world's tourist attractions can be found just a ways off the bustling main thoroughfare of Singapore's Orchard Road on the grounds of the Haw Par Villa: a theme park–style walk-through of the Ten Courts of Chinese Hell.

Haw Par Villa was originally called Tiger Balm Gardens. It was constructed in the late 1930s by brothers Aw Boon Haw and Aw Boon Par, the wealthy creators of the skin-tingling Tiger Balm ointment. The brothers built a huge private residence, but then decided to spread across their property a collection of pagodas on which figures of ancient Chinese mythology would be exhibited in colorful statue form.

As the gardens grew into a popular public picnic ground, the exhibits were expanded. A gigantic dragon was constructed, with a boat ride running through it. Visitors floated through the beast's ravenous jaws and exited seventy yards later by way of a waterfall plume out the tail. Today, Haw Par has its share of smiling Buddhas and pastoral fairy-tale scenes, but the most popular attraction of all remains the walking tour of the Courts of Hell.

The courts were originally part of the dragon structure,

but now are presented in a more hellish procession of caves. Visitors are greeted by the guardians of hell—two heavily armed, powerful demons known as Ox-Head and Horse-Face (their appearances are pretty self-explanatory). The first court is administrative: Sins are detected in a Mirror of Retribution. Then the punishment begins. Taking in a series of huge, brightly colored dioramas (using a lot of bloodred), one can see prostitutes being drowned in boiling blood, cheaters being sawn in half and flung onto a tree of knives, and those who did not listen to their parents being ground up between two huge stones. Drug addicts are grilled up against a red-hot pillar, gossipers have their tongues ripped out, and robbers have their heads and limbs sawed off. The work is done by an army of varied demons, who all seem to be enjoying themselves considerably.

Finally, sinners drink a tea that lets them forget their sins (and hopefully their dismemberment) to ready them for another attempt at an unwicked life.

TURN OFF THAT DAMNED MUSIC

Some hellish albums:
Hell by James Brown
Highway to Hell by AC/DC

Hell Freezes Over by the Eagles
Bat Out of Hell by Meat Loaf
It's Dark and Hell Is Hot by DMX
Heaven and Hell by Black Sabbath
Hell Bent for Leather by Judas Priest
Whiskey Bent and Hell Bound by Hank Williams Jr.
Hell on Earth by Mobb Depp
Hell's Ditch by the Pogues
Hell Awaits by Slayer
Alice Cooper Goes to Hell by Alice Cooper

LIKE MIKE

The great Michelangelo only painted hell once, but it was a doozy. Having completed the physically punishing task of painting the ceiling of the Sistine Chapel between 1508 and 1512, Michelangelo was summoned back to the Vatican in the early 1530s and was asked by Pope Paul III to paint the expansive wall behind the chapel's altar. The task was daunting, especially since the artist was almost sixty at the time, but he focused his considerable talents and, over a seven-year period, created a masterpiece: *The Last Judgment.*

The painting captures the moment as the Judgment begins. At top center, Christ, sitting with the Virgin Mary, is surrounded by virtuous souls and a number of saints, most of whom carry some symbol of their martyrdom (St. Lawrence with the gridiron he was burned alive on, St. Catherine with the spiked wheel she was tortured on). To the left, souls recovering their renewed bodies ascend to heaven. On the right, angels and demons battle over souls falling hellward. At the bottom of the painting, one can see details presumably drawn from Dante's work: Charon is doing his ferrying work, and hideous Minos, with his serpent coils, is ready to assign sinners their place. One of the most famous and striking images of the piece is that of a man being tugged to hell by an eager demon. The man's tortured, haunted expression indicates that he knows exactly where he is heading.

Michelangelo must have been proud of his achievement, but the toll it took on him may be evident in one telling detail. Rather than paint himself among the saved or the heaven-bound, as was the custom of artists at the time, Michelangelo portrayed himself as a wearied St. Bartholomew, who was flayed to death (he holds the suit of skin that's been beaten off him).

The artist may have felt further flayed by the reaction to the great work. Because the painting featured so many nude figures, with genitals clearly in evidence, it was decried as a work of obscenity and became an ongoing point of controversy for the church. One Vatican authority, Biagio da Cesena, said that the work was not worthy of the chapel of the pope and belonged instead in a public bath or a cheap tavern. Michelangelo responded by sending da Cesena to hell, painting his face as the face of the monstrous Minos. Soon after, a *Last Judgment* censorship campaign was launched by several cardinals, but Paul III would not oblige them. However, almost immediately after Michelangelo's death in 1564, an official campaign to cover up genitals in church paintings was begun. The artist Daniele da Volterra was brought in to apply fig leaves, draped fabric, and other *braghe* (pants) or *perizomas* (undies) to cover up naughty bits. More coverups were added by others over the centuries.

During a comprehensive cleaning and restoration of the *Last Judgment* in the 1980s and 1990s, it was decided that most of the *braghe* could not be removed without damaging the original delicate nether-regions beneath them.

GO TO WAR

Two interesting World War II propaganda films teamed Satan and Adolf Hitler as costars. In 1942's *Inflation*, the devil decides to pitch in and assist Hitler with his plan for world domination. The extremely cunning devil (played by Eddie Arnold) suggests that instead of trying to defeat the bothersome United States in a battlefield showdown, the true path to victory is through the American pocketbook. If Americans can be persuaded to forget about saving for the war effort and to begin spending indiscriminately, the U.S. economy will tumble and Germany will prevail. The Americans (including a dry, non-bathing-suited Esther Williams) are indeed tempted by the devil and begin raiding their nest eggs to make big-ticket impulse purchases. Things look dark for the big-spending United States, but the citizenry comes to its senses just in time—thanks to inspirational words from F.D.R. (playing himself by way of archival footage). Note: As the devil, Eddie Arnold was demonstrating some spiritual range here—just the year before, he was on the other side, battling the devil (in the person of Walter Huston) as the star of *The Devil and Daniel Webster*.

In *The Devil with Hitler*, a short film also produced in 1942, the devil is in danger of losing his job to Hitler, who has quite obviously made a hell of Earth. Satan's job security can only be maintained if he can entice the führer to spoil a perfect evil record by committing an act of goodness. Thus the devil goes to work on Hitler, who is chiefly seen gallivanting with Mussolini and an Asian general named Suki Yaki. Less than hilarious slapstick ensues.

QUEL HELL SELLS

The word pictures of hell that Dante Alighieri created in the *Inferno* were powerful enough to make that work a classic in just about any translation, but many of his images were made visually explicit in nineteenth-century editions of the book, thanks to the work of illustrator Gustave Doré. Doré (1832–1883) began his career working as a teenage phenom, creating caricatures for Parisian magazines, and designing striking engravings for a wide variety of books. Doré's style mixed romanticism and realism, and as his success grew, he sought to match his talents to the work he felt screamed out most for a fully illustrated edition, Dante's *Divine Comedy*. The top publishers in Paris all rejected the idea as being cost-prohibitive, but Doré went ahead and created scores of full-page engravings to cover the infernal journey, then essentially self-published a first edition of the work. It was a smash success, causing one publisher who had rejected the idea as a non-moneymaker to send the artist a famously apologetic telegram: "I am an ass."

The *Inferno* wasn't Doré's only trip to hell. He also illustrated a successful edition of *Paradise Lost*, and came up with some disturbing, detailed visions of the Last Judgment for a popular illustrated version of the English Bible.

COME ON IN

The most familiar works of French sculptor Auguste Rodin may be his hunky head scratcher, *The Thinker*, and his couple in the midst of passionate embrace-with-reach-around, *The Kiss*. Less well known is the fact that these two images were originally meant to be a part of hell.

Both *The Thinker* and *The Kiss* were designed to be figures incorporated within Rodin's massive masterpiece, a rendition of the entryway that no one wants access to, *The Gates of Hell*. The piece was to be a doorway for a museum that was never built, a museum of decorative arts in Paris. In 1880, Rodin received a commission for the work, which was to draw upon characters, images, and events from Dante's *Inferno* (the commission was a huge boost to the career of the not-yet-famous sculptor). Rodin dove in and began his complicated work process for the sculpture, which was intended to be exhibited in 1889 at the International Exposition in Paris, a celebration that marked the one-hundredth anniversary of the French Revolution, and the same shindig for which the Eiffel Tower was constructed. But the elaborate endeavor became an ongoing work-in-progress for Rodin, and was not finished to his satisfaction at the time of his death in 1917.

At first, as Rodin sketched out his concept for the *Gates* and began constructing small models, he seems to have wanted to follow a fairly literal approach to depicting Dante's narrative. The figures for the piece included a number of characters pulled directly from the poem, including Paolo and Francesca, a pair of adulterous lovers who Dante had encountered in the second circle of hell. But as Rodin progressed on the *Gates*, he decided to take a less direct approach, creating a work with a more abstract relationship to Dante's hell. Eventually, almost all recognizable characters from the poem were removed (some for very good reason—Rodin had realized that his original Paolo and Francesca looked like they were having much too enjoyable a make-out session to be tormented denizens of damnation).

One infernal figure that remained was Dante himself, the muscular Thinker, who had a central position above the doors either to reflect upon the creation of his epic work or—in the role of any-soul—to ponder his fate in the afterlife.

As progress on the *Gates* slowed, Rodin liberated some of the figures he had designed and allowed them a life of their own. Dante's figure became a full-size bronze of *The Thinker* (sometimes referred to as *The Poet*). And Paolo and Francesca became the more generic, but no less erotically charged, full-size marble couple of *The Kiss*.

Today much of Rodin's intermediary work for *The Gates of Hell*, along with one of its original castings, can be viewed at the Musée Rodin in Paris.

In 1987, Rodin had one more slightly less significant brush with devilish artwork. A photograph of his sculpture *Eternal Idol* was used as album cover art by the band Black Sabbath. The sculpture is generally considered to be a masterful evocation of (nude) tenderness and sensuality. But the album, recorded by an unsteady, Ozzy-less Sabbath lineup (presumably non-nude), is generally considered a middling metal effort.

DEVIL MADE THEM DO IT

In medieval hell legends, sometimes the only way for a woman to win back her husband's damned soul was to submit to the devil's carnal desires. A few centuries later, devil deals were viewed in a similarly overheated fashion by way of the 1970s porno film *The Devil in Miss Jones*, in which a woman who has committed suicide can win her soul back only by revisiting earth and making carnal amends with all those she has sinned against.

HELL-TRIPPER

Sure your theologians, artists, and visionaries can prattle on about what they think hell looks like and what they think goes on there. But where are the lab studies and fieldwork to back them up? What would happen if a calmly analytical, cold-eyed scientist could descend on a fact-finding research survey of hell and report back to us?

The answers can be found in the writings of Emanuel Swedenborg, a brilliant eighteenth-century scientist who in his later years applied his scientific approach to a powerfully original form of spirituality. He's often referred to as a mystic, and philosopher Immanuel Kant essentially wrote off Swedenborg's theology as a pile of nonsense. Mumbo jumbo may be in the eye and ears of the beholder, but in works such as *The New Jerusalem*, *The True Christianity*, and *Heaven and Hell*, Swedenborg coolly and logically lays out an intricately detailed, step-by-step explanation of his neo-Christian cosmos. And in that latter work he also provides a travelogue of hell that is as eye-opening as Dante's and as well organized as any AAA road guide.

Swedenborg should be allowed plenty of space in history books regardless of his hell-related work. His name doesn't have the cachet of an Isaac Newton or an Albert Einstein, but his scientific accomplishments are truly awesome. In the first couple of decades of the 1700s, Swedenborg was gobbling up everything he could learn about mathematics, physics, biology, and chemistry. It seems that as quickly as he was able to absorb knowledge, he was able to put it to use in all sorts of ingenious inventions and startling hypotheses. He started out by impressing the military-minded King Charles XII of Sweden by coming up with breakthrough metallurgical processes and designing machines that could move warships over land. He went on to pioneer advances in mining, and sketched out working designs for such machines of the future as the submarine and the airplane.

Swedenborg developed a theory of molecular structure that would largely prove to be accurate as modern science advanced. The same goes for his theories on the function of the spinal cord. He pushed forward the fields of economics, geography, and astronomy. He designed a more effective chimney for Swedish households. (And from the letters of friends and family, we know that he was well liked, raising the important question: Is there anything more truly depressing than a brilliant, beloved overachiever?)

But Swedenborg's empirical, objectively scientific approach to the world changed dramatically around Easter 1744, when, after a series of what seem to have been violent, hallucinatory fever dreams (bad ham?), he devoted his life to a pursuit of spiritual truths.

The amazing, distinctive element in Swedenborg's religious writing is that he is speaking as a scientist and observer who has been offered a firsthand glimpse into the inner workings of the cosmos. He came to believe that, while in a kind of trance, he was visited by angelic spirits who could whisk him through the spirit realm, acting as helpful docents in fielding all his questions. The man of science must have known that such a career shift would invite ridicule from his contemporaries (indeed, he got some ridicule, but confusion, disinterest, and "just humor the old guy" seem to have been more common responses to his later work). Then again, a good deal of his scientific breakthroughs weren't fully understood and vindicated until centuries later, and maybe Swedenborg felt that cosmological time was on his side.

Whether or not one considers Swedenborg's spiritual means of deduction nutty, his theology is remarkably generous. He believed that the energy the universe ran on was that of love, and that God was a being of pure love and mercy. Every human was a minibattlefield for the forces of godliness and worldliness, but everyone had a chance to get to heaven.

So how did Swedenborg's hell work? Swedenborg spells it out in *Heaven and Hell*, which was originally published in Latin in 1758. Its more official English title is *Heaven and Its Wonders and Hell, from Things Heard and Seen.*

First of all, Swedenborg discovered that there was no one big Satan, but that evil was solely the work of human impulses (although there are some demonic genies that can help things along). In terms of layout, Swedenborg's hell had a lot of different sections and looks. There were caverns, jungles, deserts, and cities in ruins. These various areas of hell range in hellishness from the mild to the unspeakably dreadful (Swedenborg points out that the more horrid regions are in the north of hell, while the milder areas are in the south).

As for a ticket in, Swedenborg said that no soul was sent to hell by an angry God as a form of punishment. Instead, the soul itself, if it were evil enough, would turn away from God's love and choose hell for itself. Swedenborg's reasoning here was pretty tight: A soul that had overindulged in worldly evils would be jonesing for more of those evils, and so would pick what it saw as the pleasures of hell over the perceived lack of action in heaven. The problem was that on earth, evil was balanced out by God's love. The ability to experience pleasure and to love living a nasty life came from some small spark of goodness within even the most wicked soul. But when that jonesing bad soul went to hell in search of more kicks, it discovered that it was in a realm of pure evil, unchecked or balanced by God's love. Then all that evil that had once seemed like a good time was felt as a tormenting punishment.

Swedenborg saw that the real seed of evil was self-love (as opposed to the virtues of love of the Lord and love of others). So the chief torment of hell was that one would be stuck among hideous, horrible souls that were all completely full of themselves (insert your own joke about boardrooms, co-op meetings, or Hollywood studios here). God allows such souls to torment each other because it is the best way to keep evil under control; after all, if the damned weren't bothering the hell out of each other, the madness and chaos of the place would spill into other realms. Swedenborg doesn't go into the specific ways in which the damned torment each other, because he says that such information "would be too abominable."

He does describe the appearance of the damned, though. Some have the faces of corpses; some are charred and blackened; some are disfigured with warts, ulcers, and hellish acne. Some faces have a single feature: a gaping mouth. Some have no face at all, just a bony, hairy, blank expanse. But Swedenborg explains that there is a surprising bit of God's mercy at work in hell: The damned show their horrible appearance only to those who view them by way of heavenly light (as Swedenborg does). In such instances, the hideousness of their spirit is reflected in their physical self. But if the damned stay in the darkest regions of hell, they appear to each other simply as endlessly annoying humans, rather than as deformed demons.

Swedenborg's scientific analysis helps to explain a few long-standing hell mysteries. Is there infernal fire, and does it actually burn a soul? Swedenborg concludes that the fires of hell are visible only to those, like himself, who gaze upon the place from an undamned state. The flames are a kind of hellish aura that demonstrate the power of the twisted lusts and passions contained within the place. But the souls down there don't see the flames, and aren't aware that they are burning.

And what about that curious biblical line that hell is a place where there is always "the gnashing of teeth"? Swedenborg deduces that this is the sound of all those horrible, angry, lying, hateful, self-loving souls yammering at each other. As was often the case in life, they are quite incapable of shutting the hell up.

MY HELL

GREG PROOPS

Comic, actor, "bon vivant," voice of the devil in
The Nightmare before Christmas

Hell exists. Watch MTV. Corruption disguised as coolness, wanton selfishness dressed up as self-determined youth, wasted lives displayed as inspirational role models. The end of history. That stops where video begins. The end of literacy too. The sum total of the universe boiled down to one's personal feelings, like any *Road Rules Challenge*.

MARITAL RELATIONS

The reputation of painter, poet, engraver, and illustrator William Blake (1757–1827) has been sadly anthologized down to one harmless nubbin of verse: "Tyger, tyger, burning bright. . . ." Blake was in fact one of the most radical and original artists and thinkers of his time, and nowhere is his heady iconoclasm more evident than in his hell-related work.

As a youth in London, Blake picked up a steady career path when he apprenticed at an engraver's shop, and he later developed his painting chops by studying at the Royal Academy of Arts Schools of Design. A brilliant and innovative artist, he invented the process of relief etching. But he was a blossoming poet as well, and by the early 1780s, he was working as a one-man production team, writing and illustrating his own books.

Blake considered himself a Christian, though he rejected most traditional notions of what constituted Christianity. As his writing turned toward questions of religion and philosophy, he began to develop his own distinctly personal view of good and evil, God and Satan, and paradise and damnation. These ideas were spelled out powerfully in his book *The Marriage of Heaven and Hell*.

Blake had been briefly intrigued by the writings of Emanuel Swedenborg, and even attended a Swedenborgian New Jerusalem Church, but quickly came to feel that the Swedenborgian mysticism wasn't quite mystic enough and that it ultimately endorsed the same Old Religion morality that he wanted to break free from. *The Marriage of Heaven and Hell*, which Blake worked on in the early 1790s, began as a satirical attack on Swedenborg, but eventually grew to become a working manifesto of Blake's beliefs.

For Blake, hell is not a place of punishment at all, but a place of rampant, natural, creative energy. Heaven, on the other hand, is a stultifying, imagination-crushing place of rules, regulation, and social convention. The cosmic life force that animates the universe comes in the form of "poetic genius," and institutionalized religion can't help but suppress it, if not snuff it out completely. Blake also contends that humans are not split into separate components of body and soul, but are each a singular package, with the body simply serving as the soul's means for experiencing sensual pleasure. As for good and evil, Blake says, "Good is the passive that obeys reason. Evil is the active springing from energy."

Blake doesn't just ramble on about hell; he speaks from firsthand experience. Like the works of Dante and Swedenborg before him, Blake's writing is largely constructed as a recounting of his own journey to hell. He debates the merits of heaven and hell with an angel (the pro-hell Blake wins), dines with biblical luminaries Isaiah and Ezekiel, and visits an infernal print shop (where he picks up some new acid-based printing techniques). Most significantly, Blake reports back to his readers a complete belief system of hell's residents, captured in a section of *The Marriage* titled "Proverbs of Hell." These bits of hellish wisdom range from innocuous truisms ("A fool sees not the same tree that a wise man sees") to deep stuff ("Joys impregnate. Sorrows bring forth") to some real shockers ("Prisons are built with stones of Law / Brothels with bricks of Religion"; "The head Sublime, the heart Pathos, the genitals Beauty / the hands & feet, Proportion").

The Marriage of Heaven and Hell ends with a cry of antichurch prospiritualism: "For every thing that lives is Holy."

In later works such as *The First Book of Urizen* and *The Four Zoas*, Blake further developed his own imaginative mythology. His art and writing were appreciated by a number of similarly free-thinking contemporaries (he palled around with the likes of Thom Paine and Mary Wollstonecraft), but to the public at large he was seen as a very good engraver with a bundle of eccentric ideas and personal quirks. He died poor and was buried in an unmarked grave at a public cemetery outside London. He has since been given a proper memorial in St. Paul's Cathedral.

VIEW FROM A SATAN

Mark Twain (born Samuel Clemens, 1835–1910) ranks as one of America's most gifted and significant humorists, and in monumental works such as *Tom Sawyer* and *Huckleberry Finn* he demonstrated his extraordinary talent for both celebrating and satirizing just about every aspect of American life. His sharp eye for the foibles and contradictions within American religious beliefs and social attitudes did not dim as he grew older—in fact, as his view of humanity grew darker and more pessimistic, his satire became more pointed and his targets more deeply philosophical. In two works that were not published until after his death, he took religion head on by way of giving Satan a voice. In 1897, he began work on a sympathetic portrait of the devil's childhood, *Chronicle of Young Satan*. In 1909, he created one of his darkest works, *Letters from Earth*, the letter writer in question being a cuttingly observant Satan.

This Satan begins pre-Fall, chumming about in heaven with his angelic friends Michael and Gabriel. They watch God begin his act of creation of the universe, and his grand moral experiment, an earth populated by humans. When Satan is overheard making some disparaging comments about what God considers to be his masterpiece, Satan is banished from heaven for a celestial day. He travels to earth to get a closer look at what is going on and, in a series of eleven letters to Michael and Gabriel, describes the state of humanity as wildly insane, utterly contradictory, and supremely depressing.

Twain's Satan is a wisecracking rebel, but he is certainly not a figure of ultimate evil. As a mordant observer of life on earth, Satan is particularly puzzled at the relationship between humans and heaven, noting that mortals look forward to a paradise in which they will do things they don't do very well on earth—singing, praying, and playing the harp—while they don't allow heaven to include their greatest earthly pleasure, copulation. Satan is also surprised to discover that humans themselves have invented the concept of hell—Satan had nothing to do with it. Actually, he sees something hellish in the heaven that humans strive for: "Consider the deafening hurricane of sound—millions and millions of voices screaming at once and millions and millions of harps gritting their teeth at the same time! I ask you: is it hideous, is it odious, is it horrible?"

Twain did not expect *Letters from the Earth* to be

published, joking that if it were published, it would constitute a felony. And the work did go unpublished for over fifty years after Twain's death. In 1939, Bernard DeVoto, the literary editor of Twain's estate, decided to take some of the writer's unpublished work out to the public, but Twain's daughter, Clara Clemens, would not allow *Letters* to be published, feeling it was not a true reflection of her father's feelings toward religion. After her death in 1962, the work was finally released, and spent eighteen weeks on the *New York Times* bestseller list.

KICKS

Major League Soccer teams the Chicago Fire and the Dallas Burn have a running rivalry, and at the end of each season it is settled by awarding a large trophy, the Brimstone Cup, to the team that has won the most Fire-Burn showdowns. The cup is inscribed with words from Virgil's *Aeneid*: "The more the kindled combat rises high'r, The more with fury burns the blasing fire."

ART IS HELL

The tradition of great hell artists such as Hieronymus Bosch have been carried into modern times by artists such as the New York–based Joe Coleman. Coleman allegedly began making pencil sketches of martyred saints when he was eight, and his professional work has continued to gather inspiration from the darker, bloodier side of religious themes (he's painted scenes from the book of Revelation, he was part of a "100 Artists See Satan" exhibit, and a recent collection of his work was titled "Original Sin"). Coleman's paintings may not often present the netherworld per se, focusing instead on the hellish aspects of life on earth, but his remarkably dense and detailed works, like Bosch's, feature scenarios of decay, debasement, degradation—and often quite a bit of exposed innards. His work *The Man of Sorrows*, which depicted the life of Jesus in accordance with various apocrypha, was hung at a 2001 Bosch exhibit in Rotterdam as an example of modern artists influenced by the master. Collectors have also been known to hang Coleman's work next to work by the Brueghels.

Coleman has also worked as a somewhat notorious performance artist. At a 1989 show at the Boston

Film / Video Foundation, he decided to bring a bit of literal hell to the stage by strapping dynamite to his body and blowing himself up before startled onlookers (while he was not seriously injured, he cleared out the room fast). The artistic merits of such a performance can be debated, but the Boston Police Department gave Coleman its own review: He was arrested and charged with the archaic offense of "possession of an infernal machine."

DEAR DEMON

C. S. Lewis, the twentieth-century author, medievalist, and Christian apologist, is best known to many readers as the creator of compelling fantasy fiction such as *Perelandra* and *The Chronicles of Narnia*, especially the first published work of the Narnia series, *The Lion, the Witch, and the Wardrobe*. Lewis was a master of allegory, often shaping his stories and characters to reflect Christian themes and teachings, and at other times drawing upon classic themes from ancient mythology. In his nonfiction writing (*Mere Christianity*, *Miracles*), Lewis was an open, thoughtful advocate of his own faith, and he clearly took his religion quite seriously. But in a couple of his works of fiction, he notably dropped the purely allegorical approach to take on Christian notions of good and evil both directly and humorously.

In *The Great Divorce*, Lewis presents a tale of heaven and hell that plays out like a mix of Dante's *Divine Comedy* and a particularly creepy *Twilight Zone* episode. The narrator finds himself in hell, which takes the form of a dull, dreary, seemingly endless downer of a town. The town is part of a very strange public transportation system: A bus travels from hell to heaven, and Lewis rides it among a group of hell-based tourists who are taking a day trip to paradise. In heaven, residents of hell become painfully ghostlike. They cannot fully interact with their surroundings, and their feet don't even bend the blades of grass beneath them. The bright and cheerful residents of heaven present a welcoming option for the visitors: With repentance of sins and the proper change of heart, the hell people could stay in heaven and become bright, cheerful, solid, and unghostly themselves. Lewis's *Zone*-like twist: Even with such easy entrance requirements to heaven, the busload of hell folk make all kinds of excuses why they can't stay, and they offer all sorts of rationalizations why they are better off where they came from (they're actually so stubbornly self-centered that they don't realize their hometown is hell).

In *The Screwtape Letters* (1942), an older devil named Screwtape writes to his young devil nephew Wormwood, offering advice on how the youngster may best tempt his first human, "the patient," into eternal damnation. The malevolently sagacious Screwtape has already done his time on earth, and is now serving as a prosperous functionary in hell's government (the "Lowerarchy"). His letters reflect an upside-down view of morality: "Our Father" is Satan, and "the Enemy" is God. The young devil is having a hard time corrupting his human. In fact, the patient converts to Christianity almost as soon as Wormwood's demonic temptations begin. Screwtape tells his pupil to concentrate on instigating small, slippery-slope sins rather than trying to incite one big damning act, and through his letters he offers some tricks of the trade in encouraging just about all of the seven deadly sins.

Despite the careful, evil mentoring, things don't end well for Wormwood. His patient dies a war hero and goes straight to heaven. Screwtape, feeling the sting of the great teacher let down by the crappy student, coldly informs his nephew that he will be recalled to hell, where he will promptly be eaten by his fellow demons.

Lewis allegedly found the experience of writing in a devil's voice to be highly unpleasant, but Screwtape popped up one more time in Lewis's work. In the essay

"Screwtape Proposes a Toast," the old devil addresses an after-dinner crowd to express his great pleasure with current developments in the British education system.

MODERN HELLSCAPING

For just about as long as hell has been thought of as a seriously terrifying religion-born place of eternal punishment, it's also been used as a seriously terrifying, pop culture–spawned setting for some darker moments of fiction. These days, hell remains a scarifyingly fruitful setting for the prolific and accomplished artist, writer, and filmmaker Clive Barker.

As a young playwright, Barker jumped effectively into all things hellish with *The History of the Devil*, a stage work that offers a great deal of sympathy for Lucifer. Barker's devil is true to his roots as a malevolent charmer, but he has grown weary and lonely being a heavenly outcast. He misses his angelic wings and the pleasures of flight; he even misses the days when he could hang out in friendly fashion with God. He asks for a full-scale trial—complete with opposing lawyers, subpoenaed witnesses, and a jury of souls—to prove that it's humanity's inherent evil and wickedness that have made a mess of the earth, not the devil's own messing around. If he wins, he gets back into heaven; if he loses, he's stuck overseeing the bad times on earth.

The play has been frequently performed, and had some very successful stagings at the Edinburgh Fringe Festival. Its commercial success has been aided by some satanic notoriety: When a British venue banned the play's performance in 1998, subsequent productions enjoyed sellout runs.

Barker is probably better known for his unsettling, darkly spiritual, gore-friendly books and films. An early novel, *Damnation Game*, was a reworking of the Faust myth, and his work since has ranged from the explicitly diabolical tales of his *Books of Blood* short-story collections to the creepy-as-hell goings-on in his *Abarat* series. Perhaps his most popular film has been 1987's *Hellraiser*, which he wrote and directed, basing the story on his novel, *The Hellbound Heart* (the film led to a long series of sequels that had varying input from Barker). In the movie, he envisioned a netherworld populated by sadistic, heavily leathered and studded demons known as Cenobites (the memorable lead Cenobite was a nail-skulled miscreant referred to as Pinhead). Barker envisioned an equally disturbing hell in 1990's *Nightbreed*, in which grotesquely mutated souls suffer in the depths of a netherworld as richly textured as a Hieronymus Bosch painting.

Barker has been a master of all hell trades, spreading his visions by way of paintings, comic books, television productions, and video games. In 2001, he offered damnation fans a way to actually get their hands on a piece of his hell with the release of his exquisitely horrifying Tortured Souls action figures.

MAKE IT LOOK LIKE IT HURTS

The name Luca Signorelli may not ring those freshman-art-history-required-course bells the way Michelangelo and Hieronymus Bosch do, but he deserves a mention for bringing the torments of hell to an unparalleled level of hard-to-look-at realism. The Italian Renaissance painter, technically a master of the Umbrian school, developed a keen knack for creating perspective and a stunning talent for depicting nude human anatomy. That knack and that talent were put to exceptional use in the hellscapes Signorelli created as frescoes for the Orvieto Cathedral. His hellbound sinners aren't just shuffling through the Last Judgment and their damnation; they are in contorted, tendon-straining, anatomically correct agony, and the gleefully grotesque fiends and demons that torment them are no less vivid. Michelangelo is thought to have been a fan of Signorelli's approach, and in his own work he drew upon some of Signorelli's presentations of the human form in extreme anguish.

Signorelli's work may have eventually become too real for its own good. In 1508 he was brought to the Vatican to create a fresco for the walls of the papal apartments, but was quickly dismissed so that those walls could be filled with the more harmonious, uplifting work of Raphael.

DESCENT OF THE NEBBISH

Some of Woody Allen's fans consider *Annie Hall* his best work, and the 1977 film garnered a fair amount of official recognition of excellence, picking up a Best Picture Oscar and winning Allen and cowriter Marshall Brickman an Oscar for Best Screenplay. Allen also won a Best Director award for the film. But the film's original script differed greatly from what eventually made it to the big screen. The film—originally titled *Anhedonia*, a term for the inability to experience pleasure—at one point included a number of fantasy sequences, including one in which Woody's character, Alvy Singer, Diane Keaton's Annie, and Tony Roberts as Alvy's best friend take an elevator ride with the devil down through the depths of hell.

Allen's hell, like Dante's, was divided into descending levels of wickedness, but purportedly contained some classes of sinners that Dante missed: people who say "Right on," CIA assassins, FBI informers, fast-food servers, people who try to be funny with waiters, the guy who invented double-knits, and Richard Nixon.

Allen finally did take a cinematic trip to hell in his 1997 film, *Deconstructing Harry*. Again, damnation is accessed by way of an elevator, and this time an automated voice announces to Allen's character, Harry Block, the inhabitants of each level.

Floor 5 contains subway muggers, aggressive panhandlers, and book critics.

Floor 6 is full of right-wing extremists, serial killers, and lawyers who appear on television.

Floor 7 is reserved for the media (it's announced that this floor is filled to capacity).

Floor 8 is for escaped war criminals, television evangelists, and the National Rifle Association.

Floor 9 is the lowest level. Anybody left on the elevator has to get off here.

Allen's vision of hell is decidedly Dante-esque. It is a fiery vista of pits and caverns where condemned souls—mostly nude—are whipped, chained, boiled, and prodded by muscular demons with pitchforks. One distressed fully clothed soul, with his own armed demonic attendant, identifies himself as a character worthy of the lowest level: He is the man who invented aluminum siding. Harry Block is surprised to find his own father chained up here, and is informed by a horned demon that the man is condemned to eternal suffering for acting unconscionably toward his son. Harry makes it clear that he forgives his father, and instructs the demon to take his father to heaven. The father points out that, as a Jew, he doesn't believe in heaven; he'd prefer to go to a Chinese restaurant. Harry suggests Joy Luck.

Harry Block then makes his way to the devil's inner sanctum, where the lord of darkness, played as a suave, martini-sipping swinger by Billy Crystal, divulges a couple of juicy hellish secrets. It turns out that the devil is constantly being offered jobs by earthly headhunters, and did in fact run a Hollywood studio for two years ("You can't trust those people," the devil says). The devil also lets on that hell is actually air-conditioned—the better to destroy the ozone layer.

After the devil pours Harry a drink of tequila from his private bar, he offers this toast: "To evil—it keeps things humming."

FINAL NOTE

What might we say to summarize this survey of the netherworld?

Perhaps this:

Hell is real.

What kind of "real" is still, of course, very much a matter of debate. A geographical place. A human idea. A realm of spirit. A pop-cultural conceit.

Unfortunately, it does not do to propose that everyone can simply believe in the hell of their choice: Those who maintain that hell is a very real place of damnation certainly do not excuse unbelievers from the flames, and those who see hell as a realm of mythology are not likely to concede any real fiery damnation to others.

But still, it seems utterly foolish to suggest that the

place does not exist. Real or mythological, it is a significant, undeniable presence in our religion and our poetry, in our morality and our museums, in our philosophy and our entertainment, in our language and our dreams.

However and whatever one thinks of hell, it has been a powerful force in countless human lives, and it has undeniably shaped human history.

We leave it as we approached it—with both fear and fascination.

> *Long is the way and hard,*
> *that out of hell leads up to light.*
> —John Milton, *Paradise Lost*

BIBLIOGRAPHY

Augustine, Saint. *City of God*. Henry Bettenson, trans. (New York: Viking, 1972).

Augustine, Saint. *Confessions*. Henry Chadwick, trans. Oxford World's Classics (Oxford and New York: Oxford University Press, 1998).

BBC. "Fire Devastates Saatchi Artworks." BBC News, UK edition. http://news.bbc.co.uk/1/hi/entertainment/arts/3748179.stm (accessed May 26, 2004).

Barnstone, Willis and Marvin Meyer, eds. *The Gnostic Bible* (Boston: Shambhala, 2003).

Bede. *Ecclesiastical History of the English People*. Penguin Classics (New York: Penguin Books, 1991).

Beecher, Edward. *History of Opinions on the Scriptural Doctrine of Retribution* (New York: D. Appleton, 1878).

Bernstein, Alan E. *The Formation of Hell* (Ithaca, N.Y.: Cornell University Press, 1993).

Blake, William. *The Marriage of Heaven and Hell* (Oxford and New York: Oxford University Press, 1975).

Bloom, Harold. *Bloom's BioCritiques: Dante Alighieri* (Northborough, Mass.: Chelsea House, 2003).

Bodin, Jean. *On the Demon-Mania of Witches* (Toronto: Centre for Reformation and Renaissance Studies, 1995).

Boguet, Henry. *Examen of Witches* (1929; reprint, Whitefish, Mont.: Kessinger, 2003).

Braudel, Fernand. *A History of Civilizations* (New York: Allen Lane and Penguin Press, 1994).

Broderick, R. C. *The Catholic Encyclopedia* (Nashville: Thomas Nelson, 1987).

Brown, Lesley, ed. *The New Shorter Oxford Dictionary* (Oxford and New York: Oxford University Press Clarenden Press, 1993).

Buhler, Rich. "Background on the Drilling to Hell Story." http://www.truthorfiction.com/rumors/d /drilltohellfacts.htm (accessed January 20, 2005).

Crompton, Samuel Willard. *Spiritual Leaders and Thinkers: Emanuel Swedenborg* (Northborough, Mass.: Chelsea House, 2005).

Dalley, Stephanie. *Myths from Mesopotamia* (Oxford and New York: Oxford University Press, 1998).

de Plancy, J. A. S. Collin. *Dictionary of Demonology* (New York: Philosophical Library, 1965).

de Plancy, J. A. S. Collin. *Dictionary of Witchcraft* (New York: Philosophical Library, 1965).

Destiny Church. "The Hell House Outreach Kit." http://www.godestiny.org/ (accessed February 10, 2005).

Dharma, Krishna. *Mahabharata* (Badger, Calif.: Torchlight, 1999).

Encyclopedia of World Religions: Judaism, Christianity, Islam, Buddhism, Zen, Hinduism, Prehistoric & Primitive Religions (London: Phoebus Publishing Company; London: Octopus Books Limited, 1975; distributed by Crescent Books, NY).

Faulkner, Raymond O., ed. *The Ancient Egyptian Book of the Dead* (Austin: University of Texas Press, 1990).

Ginzburg, Carlo. *The Night Battles* (Baltimore: Johns Hopkins University Press, 1992).

Graham, Billy, and Richard N Ostling. "Of Angels, Devils, and Messages from God," *Time* (November 15, 1993).

Grant, Michael. *History of Rome* (New York: Scribner, 1978).

Guarlnick, Peter. *Searching for Robert Johnson* (New York: Plume, 1998).

Guazzo, Francesco Maria. *The Compendium Maleficarum: The Montague Summers Edition*, Dover edition (New York: Dover, 1988).

Gussow, Mel. "Woody Allen Fights Anhedonia." *New York Times* (April 20, 1977).

Hanson, J. W. *The Bible Hell* (Boston: Universalist, 1888).

Hathaway, Nancy. *The Friendly Guide to Mythology: A Mortal's Companion to the Fantastical Realm of Gods, Goddesses, Monsters, and Heroes* (New York: Winokur/Boates Book, Viking, 2001).

Heitz, Lisa Hefner. *Haunted Kansas: Ghost Stories and Other Eerie Tales* (Lawrence: University Press of Kansas, 1998).

Hell Blues Festival Web site, "Hell Blues." http://www.hellblues.com/hbf/english/historie.html (accessed September 14, 2004).

Hell, Michigan, USA Web site, "History." http://www.hell2u .com/about.html (accessed January 29, 2005).

Hell's Gate Airtram Web site, "History." http://www.hellsgateairtram.com/hga.history.html (accessed December 19, 2004).

Henson, Mitch, ed. *Lemegeton: The Complete Lesser Key of Solomon* (Jacksonville, Fla.: Megatron, 1999).

Hollywood Hellhouse official Web site, "Hollywood Hellhouse." http://www.hollywoodhellhouse.com/PRESS (accessed February 10, 2005).

Holmes, George. *The Oxford History of Medieval Europe* (Oxford and New York: Oxford University Press, 1988).

Holy Bible, King James Version (Nashville: Gideons International, 1988).

Holy Bible, New Revised Standard Edition (Grand Rapids, Mich.: Zondervan Bible Publishers), 1989.

Institoris, Henricus. *The Malleus Maleficarum of Heinrich Kramer and James Sprenger* (New York: Dover, 1971).

James, M. R., trans. *The Apocryphal New Testament* (Oxford: Clarendon, 1924).

Jewish Encyclopedia. "Sheol." http://www .jewishencyclopedia.com/ (accessed November 19, 2004).

Joe Coleman's official Web site, "About Joe Coleman." http://www.joecoleman.com/ (accessed 2003).

John Paul II, Pope, "General Audience." Vatican: Holy See. http://www.vatican.va/holy_father/johnpaulii /audiences/1999/documents/hf_jp-ii_aud_28071999 _cn.html (accessed November 15, 2004).

Johnson, Paul. *The Civilization of Ancient Egypt* (New York: HarperCollins, 1998).

Kennedy, Bud. "Devil Is in the Debate in Small Town." *Fort Worth Star-Telegram* (September 9, 2003).

Kohl, Benjamin, ed. *On Witchcraft: An Abridged Translation of Johann Weyer's De Praestigiis Daemonum* (Asheville, North Carolina: Pegasus, 1998).

Kors, Alan C. and Edward Peters. *Witchcraft in Europe, 1100–1700: A Documentary History* (Philadelphia: University of Pennsylvania Press, 1972).

Kovacs, Maureen Gallery, trans. *The Epic of Gilgamesh* (Palo Alto: Stanford University Press, 1989).

LaVey, Anton Szandor and Burton H. Wolfe. *The Satanic Bible* (New York: Avon, 1976).

Le Normand-Romain, Antoinette. "The Gates of Hell." http://www.musee-rodin.fr (accessed February 13, 2005).

Leary, Alex. "Mayor Banishes Satan from Inglis," *St. Petersburg Times* (November 29, 2001).

Leeming, David Adams. *The World of Myth: An Anthology* (Oxford and New York: Oxford University Press, 1990).

Lenburg, Jeff. *The Encyclopedia of Animated Cartoons* (New York: Facts on File, 1991).

Levy, Leonard W. *Blasphemy: Verbal Offense against the Sacred, From Moses to Salman Rushdie* (New York: Knopf, 1993).

Lewis, C. S. *The Screwtape Letters* (San Francisco: HarperSanFrancisco, 2001).

Lost Books of the Bible and the Forgotten Books of Eden (World Bible, 1968).

Lucretius. *On the Nature of Things: De Rerum Naturata*, Anthony Esolen, ed. and trans. (Baltimore: Johns Hopkins University Press, 1995).

MacGregor, S. L., ed. *The Goetia: The Lesser Key of Solomon the King* (Boston: Weiser Books, 1995).

Malan, Dan. *Gustave Doré: Adrift on Dreams of Splendor* (St. Louis, Mo.: Malan Classical Enterprises, 1995).

Mannix, Daniel P. *The Hellfire Club* (New York: I Books, 2001).

Matsunaga, Daigan. *The Buddhist Concept of Hell* (New York: Philosophical Library, 1971).

McCloy, James F. and Ray Miller. *The Jersey Devil* (Wallingford, Pa.: Middle Atlantic, 1979).

Milton, John. *Paradise Lost*. John Leonard, ed., Penguin Classics (New York: Penguin, 2003).

Morgan, Genevieve and Tom Morgan. *The Devil: A Visual Guide to the Demonic, Evil, Scurrilous, and Bad* (San Francisco: Chronicle, 1996).

O'Donovan, Oliver, ed. *From Irenaeus to Grotius: A Sourcebook in Christian Political Thought, 100–1625* (Grand Rapids, Mich.: Wm. B. Eerdmans, 2000).

Oesterreich, Traugott K. *Possession and Exorcism: Among Primitive Races, in Antiquity, the Middle Ages, and Modern Times* (New York and Cleveland: Causeway, 1974).

Olver, Lynne, ed. The Food Timeline. "History Notes: Cake." http://www.foodtimeline.org/foodcakes.html (accessed September 29, 2004).

Pagels, Elaine. *The Gnostic Gospels* (New York: Vintage, 1989).

Pagels, Elaine. *The Origin of Satan* (New York: Vintage, 1996).

Paget, Mindie. "Building's Demolition a Mystery." *Lawrence Journal-World* (March 30, 2002).

Panati, Charles. *Sacred Origins of Profound Things* (New York: Penguin Arcana, 1996).

Parrinder, Geoffrey. *World Religions: From Ancient History to the Present* (New York: Facts on File, 1971).

Partridge, Burgo. *A History of Orgies: Lost Treasures* (Basingstoke: Prion 2002).

Peterson, Joseph H., ed. *The Lesser Key of Solomon* (Boston: Weiser, 2001).

Pinsky, Robert. A new verse translation of *The Inferno of Dante* (New York: Farrar, Straus and Giroux, 1994).

Plato. *The Collected Dialogues of Plato*. Edith Hamilton, ed. (Princeton, N.J.: Princeton University Press, Bollingen Series, 1961).

Powers, John. *A Concise Encyclopedia of Buddhism* (Oxford: OneWorld, 2000).

Rawlings, Maurice S. *To Hell and Back: Life after Death: Startling New Evidence* (Nashville: Thomas Nelson, 1993).

Remy, Nicholas. *Demonolatry* (1929; reprint, Whitefish, Mont.: Kessinger, 2003).

Rinehart, David Glenn. E-mail correspondence with the authors. March 6, 2005.

Robinson, James M., ed. *The Nag Hammadi Library* (San Francisco: HarperCollins, 1990).

Rowell, Geoffrey. *Hell and the Victorians* (Oxford: Clarendon, 1974).

Russell, Jeffrey Burton. *The Prince of Darkness: Radical Evil and the Power of Good in History* (Ithaca, N.Y.: Cornell University Press, 1988).

Saggs, H. W. F. *Peoples of the Past: Babylonians* (Norman, Okla.: University of Oklahoma Press, 1995).

Scot, Reginald. *The Discoverie of Witchcraft* (New York: Dover, 1989).

Seligmann, Kurt. *Magic, Supernaturalism, and Religion: A History of Magic and Its Influence on Western Civilization* (New York: University Library, Grosset & Dunlap, 1968).

Shaw, George Bernard. *Man and Superman* (New York: Penguin, 2001).

Sinistrari, Ludovico. *Demoniality* (1927; reprint, Whitefish, Mont.: Kessinger, 2003).

Smith, John E., et al., eds. *A Jonathan Edwards Reader* (New Haven: Yale University Press, 1995).

Stone, I. F. *The Trial of Socrates* (reprint, New York: Anchor, 1989).

Swedenborg, Emanuel. *Heaven and Its Wonders and Hell: From Things Seen and Heard* (New York: Swedenborg Foundation, standard ed., 1995).

Taylor, Gordon Rattray. *Sex in History* (New York: Harper & Row, 1973).
Thayer, Thomas. *The Origin and History of the Doctrine of Endless Punishment* (Boston: Universalist, 1855).

Thompson, Stephen P. *Turning Points in World History: The Reformation* (San Diego: Greenhaven, 1999).

Thurman, Robert. *The Tibetan Book of the Dead* (New York: Bantam, 1993).

Towers, Eric. *Dashwood: The Man and Myth* (Bath: Crucible, 1987).

Tremmel, William C. *Dark Side: The Satan Story* (St. Louis, Mo.: CBP Press, 1987).

Turner, Alice K. *The History of Hell* (New York: Harcourt Brace, 1993).

Twain, Mark. *Letters from the Earth: Uncensored Writings* (New York: Perennial Classics, 2004).

Waisman, Michael. "About Mark Twain." http://www.geocities.com/swaisman (accessed February 21, 2005).

Werner, Alice. *Myths and Legends of the Bantu* (London: Frank Cass, 1968).

CHUCK CRISAFULLI, a writer and journalist, and **KYRA THOMPSON**, an Emmy-nominated documentary filmmaker, have collaborated previously on a variety of film scripts, teleplays, and series treatments. Crisafulli is the author of two nonfiction books, *Teen Spirit* and *Moonlight Drive*. As a freelance journalist, he has covered pop culture for the *Los Angeles Times*, the *Hollywood Reporter*, and *Rolling Stone*, and he was a contributing editor with *Option* magazine. Thompson's award-winning and -nominated documentary work includes *Dying to Tell the Story*, a film about war journalists, and *The Good, the Bad, and the Beautiful*, a history of women in film. Crisafulli and Thompson both live in California.